MAGAZINE WRITING TODAY

Magazine Writing Today

by

JEROME E. KELLEY

A Writer's Digest Book
Cincinnati, Ohio

Published by
Writer's Digest Books,
9933 Alliance Rd.,
Cincinnati, Ohio 45242

Library of Congress Catalog Number PN4781.R84
International Standard Book Number 911654-52-6

Copyright© 1978, Writer's Digest

Printed and bound in the United States of America

Contents

A look at the fast-paced world of magazine publishing and where the freelance writer fits in. How is the market changing? Is your environment important? Should you be a specialist or generalist writer? Finding time to write.

A breakdown of the most common and easiest to sell magazine articles. Also discusses types of magazines and what types of articles they publish (and why).

Whether to allow the interviewee final approval of the article.

Introduction

In February, 1975, *Reader's Digest* published one of my stories, "The Pied Piper of 'A' Company" as its First Person Award. A scant day after its publication, I was being buttonholed by people in the small Vermont town where I spend a good deal of my time, all asking, "How do *I* go about writing a *Reader's Digest* First Person Award story?" Within a week, my mailbox was stuffed full of letters asking the same question.

Because so many people were interested, it was obvious to me that here was the subject for another story, so in a few hours I rapped out an article, "How to Win the *Reader's Digest* First Person Award" and shipped it off to WRITER'S DIGEST. This story was published and in short order I wrote two more articles on writing for WD.

After 25 years as a writer, I was beginning to think about the actual process of writing again and this thinking led directly to the idea for *Magazine Writing Today*. It occurred to me that there are many people who have every qualification for becoming a writer, but need only encouragement and direction to make a go of it.

If you are one of those people who want to be a freelance writer, congratulations! You couldn't have picked a better profession. Besides needing writers for staff jobs, editors of thousands of magazines are impatiently waiting for *your* words. What's the pay? It depends on the market—and you—but I've made $1,000 an hour and on a few occasions $100 a minute. This is far from being a record, though. I know of one writer who became a full-fledged millionaire by selling a single 2,500-word story. Burt Zollo, writing under the name of Bob Norman, sold Hugh Hefner a piece for the first issue of *Playboy* for $400. Hefner didn't have the money, so Zollo took his payment in stock, which, in time, made him a millionaire. (Let me hasten to add that this doesn't happen every day, though.)

Magazines today are in a constant state of change. From the first attempts at magazine publishing—described by Alexander Pope as "upstart collections of dullness," they have been on the move, searching for new and better formats and writing styles that will help them attract more readers and advertisers. Today's magazine writers find there are few story subjects out of bounds. Indeed, they have a freer hand today than in years past—when it just wasn't vogue to knock the establishment. Watergate and other investigative stories have opened the door to the probing, digging style now popular.

After years of dominance by big, general-interest magazines such as *Life* and *Look,* the specialized magazine is just now coming of age. Browse through WRITER'S MARKET and you'll find that for every subject—from assembly engineering to graphology to skateboarding—there's a special-interest magazine. There are still general magazines with a broad range of acceptable subject matter, but these publications are usually aimed not at the mass population, but rather a special-interest editorial group such as college-educated readers, feminist women, chauvinist men, or people living in certain geographic areas.

More than 300 new magazines get their start each year and nearly all of them are desperately in need of dependable, talented writers to fill their pages with words.

So how do you become one of these selling writers? This is a tough question. You could approach a working writer and ask for his advice, but I doubt if you'd receive a satisfactory answer—not because writers are rude to nonwriters, but because the pros are usually too busy writing to give much thought to the actual process involved. Most learned their journeyman skills through trial and error and have long since forgotten the trials and tribulations of their apprenticeships. To them, writing has become almost a reflex action—idea, market choice, research, interview, write, sell.

My own journey toward becoming a professional writer is, I suspect, fairly typical. My first literary attempt was not!

It happened during my sophomore year at Montpelier (Vermont) High School, when the principal was fired. It just so happened that the apple of my youthful eye was his daughter, so I rose to his defense as Zola did for Dreyfus.

My *J'accuse* was a letter to the editor of the *Montpelier Evening Argus,* the then local newspaper. It execrated the school board members in no uncertain terms, raised some rather serious questions about their sanity and their parentage and, as a final fillip, called for the students to strike in protest. The letter was published in its scorching entirety and that evening, when I arrived home, I was flagged off to bed sans supper.

The next morning when I arrived at school, the students gave a series of ragged cheers. It was obvious that I had been anointed as the Moses who would lead them out of their classroom Egypt. Suddenly, a cry came from the rear of the adolescent mob. "Let's march on the State House!"

When we arrived at the State House, the students pushed me up its broad steps.

"Speech! Speech! Speech!" came the chant. For the next ten minutes my overripe rhetoric invested our principal with the wisdom of Solomon, the scholarship of Suetonius, the patience of Job and the saintliness of Mark, Matthew, Luke and John combined. Fact of the matter was, I hardly knew the guy.

As my oratory soared, I noticed several reporters furiously jotting down every word.

That night, as I sought a softer spot in the mattress for my lacerated backside, it dawned on me that I had received my first lesson in writing. I had painfully learned that the written word is one of the most powerful forces in the universe and its unreasoned use will quickly lead the writer to trouble.

Over the years, there were dozens of other lessons to be learned. I learned how to generate story ideas and develop the selectivity to know which were salable. I acquired the ability to research story ideas quickly and to extract maximum mileage from minimum information. My writing improved and the time it took to get a story onto paper grew shorter. Acceptances finally outpaced rejections and I established a profitable working relationship with a number of editors.

The qualifications for becoming a writer are not very stringent. You don't need a string of college degrees and you don't have to be artistic, eccentric or young. If you are literate and curious, and possess a sense of humor and some old-fashioned self-discipline, you can easily make the grade. Matter of fact, you can be cashing manuscript checks, possibly big ones, much sooner than you think.

I'd be pretty silly, however, if I told you that writing is easy. After all, that's what this book is all about—how to make it easier!

—*Jerome E. Kelley*

1. Today's Magazine Market

The National Aeronautics and Space Administration recently contracted a writer to do a 6,000-word article on the Viking Mars Landing Program—for $24,000, which figures out to $4 a word. As a freelance magazine writer, you'll find most assignments aren't that rewarding—at least not financially. But there are numerous other rewards in store for the successful freelancer:

You will be your own boss.
You can stay in bed as long as you want.
You can take a coffee break any time you want.
You will travel to far, exotic places.
You will meet the powerful, the rich and the beautiful.
You will be surprised to learn that the word "writer" has an aphrodisiac effect on the opposite sex.

Of course, there's another side to this coin:

You will be dealing with editors who may make the most despotic boss you've ever had appear positively benevolent.
You, as a freelancer, can stay in bed as long as you want. If you stay too long, though, you'll likely starve to death in that position.
You will drink uncounted gallons of coffee during the first ten or 15 years you work as a freelancer. After that, your doctor will tell you to quit because it's aggravating your ulcer.
You will travel to far, exotic places, all right, and frequently you'll wish you hadn't. Editors will invariably send you on assignments to the sweltering tropics in the summer and the nether regions of the Arctic in the winter.
You will meet the powerful, the rich and the beautiful—and you'll be disappointed. You'll find this group contains roughly

the same number of kooks and klutzes as any other group— maybe more.

You can ignore the aphrodisiac effects of the word "writer" insofar as after 12 to 14 hours at your typewriter, you'll be too tired to do anything about it.

Obviously, these truths aren't going to discourage you because freelance writing is, with all its penalties, an exciting, stimulating, rewarding profession.

Today's Market

New magazines are among the best starting points for beginning writers because they haven't been around long enough to have established good freelance contacts. Every editor has a group of freelancers whose work is familiar to him and he counts on these writers to supply him with a steady stream of ideas and copy. Get in on the ground floor of a new magazine and you might find yourself in favor with the editor.

With circulations and advertising profits of existing magazines healthy, publishers are currently falling over themselves to launch new magazine ventures. *Folio,* the industry's trade journal that keeps watch over new and already established ventures, reports that in 1976, 334 new magazines were born, with the biggest categories being regional and consumer/special interest publications.

These magazines, as mentioned in the introduction, are becoming more and more specialized, either in the type of subject matter they cover, or the type of audience they attract. Some magazines limit themselves to editorial matter on a limited subject, such as *Progressive Architecture, Skiing Trade News* and *Family Pet.* Others limit their editorial contents to material of interest to a specific audience—as do retirement magazines, men's magazines, and magazines for people who live in apartments. For these publications, the subject range for articles can be much broader, as long as the piece is slanted specifically toward that particular group of readers.

Payment you'll receive for magazine articles varies greatly. In some cases, payment will be only a few dollars; in others, payment may go as high as $4,000 and up. Of course, the amount of money you'll make depends on how much you write and for what markets.

According to most experts, somewhere between 60,000 and 100,000 magazines are currently being published, with 16,000 in the United States alone.

Let's forget the rest of the world and just look at the United States. If every magazine in the country—weeklies and monthlies—publishes 12 stories a month this means a staggering total of 2,304,000 magazine articles appear every year.

Of these 2,304,000 articles, probably 70 to 90% are written by freelancers. Using the conservative figure of 70%, this leaves you with 1,612,800 opportunities every year for getting a manuscript check.

Too Busy to Write?

To break into this growing magazine market, you must first stop talking about becoming a writer and start writing.

Writing, after all, is no different from any other human endeavor. Proficiency comes with practice. Theory can be gained from reading books such as this one, taking writing courses or talking with other writers, but, in the final analysis, the one and only way an aspiring writer will learn to write is by actually writing.

Frequently, the beginning writer will write spasmodically—an hour one week, two hours the next, and perhaps, not at all the next. The excuse is always pretty much the same:

"Write? I can't write regularly! I'm too busy."

Take a closer look at this excuse and you'll see that's exactly what it is—an excuse. The majority of today's employers require from an employee 37 1/2 hours each week, 50 weeks each year, with about eight paid holidays annually. So, even if you're employed by a relatively unenlightened company, you're actually working only 49 weeks, or 1,837 1/2 hours. Subtract this from the number of hours in each year and you'll have 6,922 1/2 hours. Now, for each day subtract seven hours for sleeping, two hours for eating, and three hours for watching the tube. This leaves 2,542 hours of net unoccupied time. Out of this we'll be generous and give you 1,542 hours for social activities.

You're now left with a measly 1,000 hours. For our purposes, we'll assume you are a plodding researcher, so we'll give you 500 hours to perform this important function. This leaves you with only 500 hours for actual writing.

What can you do with 500 hours when you're an excruciatingly slow writer who can wring only a single, double-spaced typescript page out of your Model 12 Underwood in an hour?

The answer is: You can multiply. Roughly 250 words fit on a typed page so, if you multiply 250 x 500 you arrive at the final figure of 125,000 words per year, which equals 50, 2,500-word magazine articles or two thin books.

Now what was that you said about not having the time to write?

Obviously, time *isn't* the problem. It's discipline. You must have discipline and guts to sit down, face an empty piece of paper and write. If you can do this regularly, the odds on your becoming a writer are quite high.

If all this preaching seems a little too pat, consider the case of one of the most prolific writers in the English language, Anthony Trollope.

A contemporary of Dickens, Eliot and Thackeray, Trollope approached the craft of writing almost casually, frequently comparing himself to a cobbler, an upholsterer and an undertaker. To him, writing was like any other job; putting words on paper was not much different from stitching leather. Trollope always maintained that his real career was with the British Postal Service where he rose from clerk to number three executive. (The idea for the street-corner mailbox was his.) In addition to his work, he was an inveterate clubman and a good family man with a passion for fox hunting. During his lifetime, he turned out the staggering total of 47 novels, five travel books, and countless magazine articles.

How did he accomplish this Byronic feat? Discipline! Every morning at five, Trollope would arise and drink his tea. At five-thirty, he would sit at his desk for a half hour reading and revising his previous day's output. Precisely at six, he started writing. For the next three and one-half hours, he turned out 1,000 words every hour with a watch in front of him to ensure he was meeting his quota. At nine-thirty he ate a large Victorian breakfast, then left for his demanding job. Though he traveled all over the world, his daily writing routine never varied.

Many of Trollope's friends, including Henry James, continually chided him for his rigidity, but he had an answer: "Nothing surely is so potent as a law that may not be disobeyed. It has the force of the water drop that hollows stone."

Were Trollope alive today, he'd have the last laugh. Many of his works are still in print and *Barchester Towers, The Last Chronicle of Barset* and the six Palliser volumes are enjoying sales that almost invest them with bestseller status.

Finding Privacy

Another favorite excuse for not writing is environment.

A beginning writer, who lived in New York City, recently complained that the bustle of the metropolis was so distracting he couldn't write. He decided to remove himself to a rural area in Idaho where he was certain the muse would move him.

Later when I was in Idaho on assignment for a large outdoor magazine, a young lady told me the tranquility of her home state was smothering her creativity as a writer. As soon as she'd saved enough money, she was heading for the Big Apple where she was certain she'd find the fuel to fire her creative furnace.

Neither of these people will ever become writers. While there are thousands of stories waiting to be written in New York City, there are just as many in Idaho. Both were using their environments as an excuse *not* to write.

Too many writers believe that in order to be successful, they must live in Minorca, Marrakech, Paris, the Seychelles, or on some sunny Caribbean isle. This would be fine if writers who went off to these far places actually enhanced their productivity, but generally, the opposite happens. Instead of pursuing their writing, expatriate writers have a tendency to pursue just about everything else—big game, deep sea fishing, the local men or maidens, or the products of nearby distilleries. When not engaged in these activities, they fritter away large amounts of time hobnobbing with the local nabobs.

After a few months or years, depending on how long their money holds out, they return quietly to their home shore and resume writing. It has cost these writers large sums of money to learn that there is no place in this wide, wide world where writing is *easy*. There are, however, certain areas where writing is much smoother, for a reason you might not suspect.

Some years ago it dawned on me that my home state, Vermont, was quite literally infested with writers and has been since the last 1800s. What was it that had attracted such literary luminaries as Rudyard Kipling (who wrote *The Jungle Books, Day's Work, The Seven Seas,* and *Captains Courageous* during his five-year residence at Brattleboro), Pearl Buck, Sinclair Lewis, Dorothy Thompson, Bernard De Voto, Alexander Woollcott, Robert Frost, and recently, Alexander Solzhenitsyn, to the Green Mountain State?

Figuring I had the makings for an article, I went pelting about asking every writer I could find why they had chosen Vermont as the place to work. The answers were all the same: "Privacy!"

Writers appreciate the fact that taciturn Vermont Yankees treat them as equals, making no big deal about their presence and leaving them alone to write in pastoral peace and quiet.

Regardless of where or how much you write, *privacy* is the one thing you *must* have. Good writing requires intense concentration and can't be undertaken with continuing distractions. Georges Simenon, author of more than 250 books, could only face the daily chore of writing by literally shutting himself off from the world. Each morning he'd close all his curtains and hang a "Do Not Disturb" sign on the door of his study. God help anyone who had the temerity to knock on it.

Where you live doesn't have a single thing to do with writing and selling magazine articles. Writing every day and having privacy does. Remember that a lot of good writing has come out of small towns, desert islands and even jails.

Specialist or Generalist?

Unless you're blessed with a rich wife or husband to support you, by far the best and safest way to get into freelancing is to ease into it on a part-time basis. Firemen, cops, lawyers, accountants, teachers, ministers, farmers, carpenters, game wardens, dentists, golf pros, and dishwashers can all be successful "sometime" freelancers. Your present profession—whatever it may be—doesn't have anything to do with your becoming a successful writer. It may, however, have some bearing on whether you become a "specialist" or "generalist" writer.

A specialist writer confines himself to a narrow subject range, frequently his vocation or avocation. Bob Stanfield, a former Air Force and airline pilot, confines his writing solely to aviation. Harold Rood, a high school biology teacher for many years, restricts his output to animals, insects, birds and other natural science subjects. Maurice Zolatow, long associated with show business, sticks closely with show-biz personalities. Harold Blaisdell, a retired educator whose life-long hobbies have been hunting and fishing, hews closely to these two areas.

Specialist writers, while many have the skills to write about any subject, only feel comfortable when writing in the field of their choice. Rumor has it they get more enjoyment out of the craft than their generalist colleagues and find the chore of writing somewhat easier.

Geographic location is another reason why writers become specialists. Many writers like where they live, don't care about travel and have a decided aversion to racing off on assignments. Harold Blaisdell has on occasion, traveled widely to uncover material for his masterful stories and books on fishing and hunting, but I'd wager a sizable sum that 90% of his story ideas have originated within a 20 to 30 mile radius of his home in Pittsford, Vermont. Similarly, Ronald Rood has written dozens upon dozens of articles and a goodly number of books by literally finding his subject matter in his backyard in the rural hamlet of Lincoln, Vermont.

Specialist writers enjoy a big advantage over other writers: after a few years they gain the reputation of being experts in their specific fields and editors compete for their articles. Because most of their writing is directed toward a select number of magazines, they're usually on a first name basis with their editors. This makes it simple for them to get a go-ahead for a story via a letter or phone call. Specialists probably collect fewer rejection slips than other writers because they're more familiar with the restricted number of magazines in their area of interest and they know what editors want.

The drawback to specializing is that the specialist usually makes less money than his generalist brethren. This supposition is based on the fact that many specialist writers labor in mighty narrow areas. Take, for instance, a writer who specializes in writing about antiques. There are only about five publications that are regular buyers of stories on the subject: *American Collector, The Antique Trader Weekly,*

The Antiques Dealer, Antiques Gazette and *The Antiques Journal.* The highest price that any of these publications pays for a 2,500-word article is about $100, while average is $50 to $75. Assuming the writer sells two $100 features each month, his annual income would be $2,400 which is hardly a living wage. Meanwhile, the generalist writer who sells a single story to *Reader's Digest* can expect $3,000 or more.

So what's a generalist writer? He's a writer who will aim his typewriter at any target of opportunity as long as there's a manuscript check in the offing. Matter-of-fact, the bylines of generalist writers such as Harry Crews, Max Gunther, Helen Laurenson, David B. Tinnan, Ted Szulc and Geoffrey Wolff seem to pop up like mushrooms after a warm rain; you can never tell where you're going to spot one next. Generalist writers have a broader market to which they can sell their work. Similarly, they usually focus on higher paying media which publishes a much broader range of articles. Generalists also crank out stories year after year, decade after decade, while specialists quickly mine their limited lode of material and get "written out" in a few years.

The beginning writer will get more stories published and catch more manuscript checks in the process if he or she takes the generalist route. After a dozen or so sales, then—and only then—should the writer consider specializing.

Speaking only for myself, I have never specialized simply because I could not afford to. While my real interest is, and has always been in the field of outdoor writing, I could never gather enough good story ideas in this single area to keep my typewriter working fulltime. Looking over my score card, only about one-tenth of my sales have fallen into the outdoor category.

Many generalists, myself included, frequently accept assignments mighty far afield from magazine writing. Besides writing for radio and TV, I've also written a syndicated newspaper column, plus brochures for plush chalet developments in the ski country and luxury co-op apartment buildings in New York City. I've also written campaign speeches for politicians—including one gubernatorial candidate—acted as an editorial consultant for two magazines, and have been responsible for the advertising and promotion of one of the most successful syndicated TV shows in the past decade.

While handling these "extracurricular" activities, I've kept right on with my main occupation which is, of course, magazine writing.

Generalist writers occasionally catch one of these extracurricular plums that are quite juicy indeed. Harrison Salisbury, for example, picked up $50,000 plus expenses for writing the well-publicized article on America that appeared in *Esquire* during the spring of 1976. Xerox Corporation paid Salisbury for writing the article and paid *Esquire* for the space in which it ran. This experiment in subsidized writing caused considerable controversy and, as a consequence, it is doubtful if any other writer will get a shot at another $50,000 assignment like this one in the foreseeable future. It's interesting to note that Salisbury was also able to put together a book from the vast amount of material he gathered while he was on the march for Xerox.

Taking Your Time

All beginning writers worry about how fast they write—but they shouldn't, since it's better to write slowly and carefully rather than fast and sloppily. In any case, speed increases with practice. At the beginning of your freelance career, you may have to sweat blood to grind out 250 words a day, but years later, you may be rapping out ten times that many.

The productivity of some writers is staggering. The late Richard Gehman sometimes had 25 to 30 published articles on the newsstands at one time. While this in itself would seem to be a herculean feat, it almost attains the realm of impossibility when one realizes that Gehman also wrote more than 30 books during his career.

Some writers though, never develop much speed. One acquaintance is a "bleeder," a term used by writers to describe their slower colleagues. He hardly ever writes more than 600 words a day, yet he makes a very handsome living, since he writes only for the highest paying publications and sells every single word he puts on paper. He probably hasn't seen a rejection slip in 20 years. Editors love him because he gives them no cause to use their blue pencils. He never misplaces a comma!

A writer's income depends on his talent, how fast he writes and how many hours a week he's willing to spend at his craft. Luck has absolutely nothing to do with it. Some part-time freelancers make

$10,000 or more each and every year, while most seasoned pros fall into the $20,000 to $50,000 bracket. At the very top rung are front-rank magazine writers who also turn out books on a regular basis and enjoy six-figure incomes. I've a suspicion that more than a few of them are millionaires and with the way publishers have been bidding up the price of nonfiction books in recent years, their numbers are likely to increase.

2. The Article Defined

With 16,000 American magazines publishing more than two million articles on a variety of subjects each year, there must be hundreds of different types of articles, right?

Wrong. Broadly speaking, there are just two types of articles—research and nonresearch.

In the case of the nonresearch article, the writer has the knowledge and experience to write it in its entirety without resorting to outside sources. Simply stated, this type of story can be cobbled up without the writer getting off his or her duff.

Research articles, on the other hand, can involve thousands of miles of travel, weeks spent poking through dusty library stacks, and dozens of interminable interviews before the writer even sits down at his typewriter.

Obviously, it doesn't take a member of Phi Beta Kappa to figure out which type of article is most popular among writers. This does not, however, make it the most salable type of article; editors, on the whole, prefer well-researched articles, since most writers don't possess the necessary knowledge to execute the nonresearch article to the editor's satisfaction. In short, don't try to cut corners on research.

Types of Articles

To get acquainted with the types of research/nonresearch articles, take a look at the following six classifications:

The who, what, when and where article. In its basic, drab, unvarnished and undecorated form, this type of article appears in daily newspapers and is usually called a "news story." In its classic newspaper format, it gives the essential facts—the who, what, when and where—about an event or development in the simplest, most direct, compact form. Usually this type of article attempts to cover all salient details in the first graph, with succeeding copy providing details that add clarity and understanding of the event and individuals involved.

When this type of article moves from a newspaper into a magazine, a wondrous transformation takes place. Like a bud bursting into bloom or a butterfly breaking out of its cocoon, the article develops color. Places assume atmosphere and become something other than just place names; adjectives give drama to the event; active verbs give character and dimension to people. For your own edification, take a story from *Time,* edit out the adjectives and substitute passive verbs for the active ones in the story. What emerges will be a newspaper news story rather than a magazine news story.

Newspapers use this type of article almost exclusively to cover fast-breaking news. Magazines use it to cover events that happened 3,000 years ago or three hours ago. This "workhorse" of the writing profession performs well in any time frame "colored" or "uncolored."

The interpretive/investigative article. This type of article contains all the elements of the who, what, when and where article plus two other very important ingredients—why and how.

The usual point of departure for a story of this type is another story—most often a news story. This story, to most readers, may appear as an innocuous, isolated incident that has little or no relationship to any past, present or future event or development of importance. It may, however, trigger a warning signal to a perceptive writer. By tracking down "why" and "how," the persistent writer may come up with a story that could well be world-shaking. The "plumber's break-in" and resulting Watergate story is a classic example.

Investigative reporting was once upon a time the exclusive domain of newspapers, but no more. Today it is standard fare in many national magazines as well as some regional publications; just take a look inside the pages of *Texas Monthly, Harper's, New York Magazine, Time, Newsweek, Philadelphia Magazine* and *New West.*

The article of opinion. Most magazines run large numbers of this type of article under various guises and disguises. Editorials, travel articles, dining out columns, book reviews, theater reviews, and movie reviews are the most common. With the exception of editorials, some editors refer to these as "service articles." Regardless of what they are called, all articles of opinion have a single purpose: to *persuade* or *dissuade* the reader.

Conclusions inherent in these articles are usually based upon the judgment of one person, usually the writer. (The millennium isn't here yet. Some editors and publishers tell writers what to write and some writers do exactly what they are told. This Pavlovian reflex is relatively common among editorial writers.)

The how-to article. Most magazines published today regularly run "how-to" articles—how to make bread, how to lose weight, how to get a better job. How-to articles generally come in three different shapes and sizes, the first being the *what someone did* story.

In its September 1976 issue, *Smithsonian Magazine* ran an article by Karen Thure on a woman who became a founding tycoon of the multibillion-dollar beauty industry, titled "Martha Harper pioneered in the hair business." The article tells of her search for a location for her beauty parlor and the resistance she met from various building owners, who didn't want to be scandalized by "fancy women and their beauty shenanigans." But Harper persevered, opened her shop and eventually expanded with numerous franchise outlets. In short, the article was about what Martha Harper did.

The *Reader's Digest* First Person Award Story is another type of what someone did article. Virtually all the *Reader's Digest* First Person stories follow a simple formula: a problem exists; the problem intensifies; the problem is solved. Obviously, someone has to do something to solve the problem and seldom does the problem or its solution have any practical applicability to the reader.

The second type of how-to article is the *how it was done piece*— probably the most used of all formulas in trade/technical/professional journals. In its most common form, the article defines a problem facing a large number of individuals or companies and delineates how the problem was overcome. The article provides a wealth of detail so readers may put the method or technique to use in their own situations.

The final type of how-to article is the *how to do it piece,* a featured attraction in many magazines. These ubiquitous articles can be easily identified because they often carry the words "how-to" in their titles. (If they don't carry the words, they at least imply them.)

Consider, for instance, the article, "Build a No-Twist Tripod Adapter", by Parry C. Yob, in the May 1977 issue of *Petersen's Photographic Magazine.* The problem—a camera rotating on the tripod screw—is defined in the first graph and the rest of the article is devoted to an explanation of a tripod adapter that will solve this problem.

Subjects for how-to articles can be almost anything. Possible treatments include "How to Meet the Widow (or Widower) Next Door" (retirement magazines); "How to Eat Crow and Like It" (outdoor magazines); and "How to Put a Price on Your Tiddly Wink Collection" (hobby magazines).

The roundup or summary article. As the name implies, the basic purpose of this type of article is to uncomplicate. Let's assume an event occurs that generates a tremendous amount of media reportage, with many divergent views and opinions being expressed. Sometimes the chronology of the series of incidents making up the event begins to become fuzzy and loses focus. It is the job of the roundup/summary article to arrange all these incidents into a logical, coherent, sequential story—a story that makes the event easier for readers to understand.

If the event is ongoing, the roundup/summary article frequently makes a forecast of what will happen if things continue on their present course. In some cases, where aspects of the event are assumed to be well-known to readers, the summary is handled in a few graphs, with the major part of the article devoted to the forecast. Numerous roundup/summary articles, triggered by the impending energy shortage have appeared in recent years.

A simpler version of the roundup/summary article is used to present an evaluation of products, goods or services appearing on the market during a specific period of time—often, but not always, annually. Wrap-up articles on fashion, automobiles, and photographic equipment are typical examples. This type of piece is sometimes called the "laundry-list" article and is one of the easiest to write.

The profile article. People are more interested in people than anything else. They love to peer into each other's lives, absorbing the intimate and not-so-intimate details that make up the patchwork of another human being's existence—who he lives with, what he eats for breakfast, what his children think of him, what he thinks about his work.

In recent years, there has been a great proliferation of what some call "gossip" magazines—the granddaddy of which, of course, is Time Inc.'s *People,* which came into existence after surveys of *Time* indicated that the heaviest read section of that news magazine was *People*, filled with short, lively, gossipy tidbits about the famous and infamous.

Profile articles, which are the standard fare in *People* and its imitators, are not limited to this gossipy approach that merely entertains the reader, though. They also contain the other kind of profile—the educational one that teaches its reader something. Some of the best examples of the educational profile can be found on a regular basis in *The New Yorker*.

The educational profile is researched and written in a manner quite unlike the profile that is meant almost solely to entertain. *New Yorker* editors might engage one of the nation's front-rank writers to do a three-part profile on a leading symphonic conductor for example. For three months the writer researches the piece and interviews the conductor's family, friends, associates, and musicians who have played under him. Another two months are spent traveling with the conductor, sitting in on rehearsals and attending performances. Another two months are spent with the writer tying up loose ends.

When the profile appears there is little attendant publicity. Only two or three music critics mention it briefly as a beautifully written piece that should be read by all music lovers.

Does the piece help the conductor? Aside from adding luster to an already distinguished name, probably not. Does it teach the reader anything? The answer is, a great deal. Virtually every reader gains insight into the dedication and discipline that is required to become a leading conductor. Obviously, some of this information can be applied to their own areas of endeavor. More importantly, all of them gain a deeper appreciation of classical music.

Types of Magazines

Generally speaking, there are three basic types of publications:

Magazines supported by advertising.

Magazines supported by companies, associations and organizations.

Magazines supported by faith, hope and charity.

The above classifications don't have much impact on writers, except that they can give a clue to why the publication's rate of payment to writers is high, or low. (In many cases, those supported by faith and hope will have much less money to spend for the written word than those making a considerable amount of money through advertising revenues.)

Perhaps a more meaningful method of classification is by breaking them down according to audience and content, but unfortunately, categorizing magazines is like pushing a car with a tow rope. Many magazines are hybrids, mutations or permutations, making it almost impossible to stick them neatly into a single generic slot.

Classifications that follow, then, are only the most basic:

General interest magazines. Although magazines in this category are supposedly edited for general interest audiences, only a few such as *Reader's Digest* and *People* actually cut across all demographic lines. Others, such as *The New Yorker* focus on high income groups, while *Harper's Magazine* and *The Atlantic Monthly* are for the college-educated crowd. Others, such as the *National Enquirer* and *Police Gazette* appeal to the reader who shops for his magazines in the aisles of the supermarket.

Science/nature magazines. With a growing interest in conservation and science, publications in this category have been expanding in numbers as well as prosperity. While some are classified as trade journals (which will be discussed later) many are aimed at the consumer—laymen who are interested in technical and scientific developments and discoveries, applied science, and technical and scientific hobbies. Within this category, the writer will find generalist publications, such as *National Parks & Conservation Magazine,* which publishes articles not only on parks, but also historical, geological, and ecological features, too; as well as specialist publications such as *Ham Radio Magazine,* which contains material strictly of interest to amateur radio licensees and electronics experimenters.

Hobbies/leisure-time activity magazines. Name anything that occupies a person's leisure time—automobiles, travel, crafts and hobbies, airplanes, boating, gardening, photography, outdoor and indoor sports—and you'll find a whole slew of magazines on the subject, most of them with a "how-to" emphasis. See *Creative Crafts, Street Chopper, Plane & Pilot, Bicycling, American Boating, Golf Magazine, Travel and Leisure* and *Camera 35.*

Regional magazines. One of the fastest-growing genres of magazines is the regional, or city variety. And writers with good writing style and provocative article ideas will find their words are welcome here.

"One of the things that virtually all regional editors have in common is a nagging lack of available writing talent," says Brian Vachon, editor of *Vermont Life Magazine*. Prospective writers should be aware that there are four distinct types of publications in this classification: large city magazines *(Philadelphia Magazine);* state magazines *(Arizona Highways);* area magazines *(Adirondack Life, Focus/Midwest)* and Sunday supplements *(Chicago Tribune Magazine).* Regional publications such as these can become an important, well-paying outlet for much of a beginning writer's early work.

Ethnic magazines. The surprising thing about ethnic publications is that there are not more of them. Several ethnic magazines have been around for a long time, e.g., *American Dane Magazine,* born in 1920, and *Black World,* 1942. Others, such as *Nuestro* —the first monthly, national magazine for Latin Americans—are relatively new. *(Nuestro* got its start in 1977.) There isn't a large number of magazines in this category and not all ethnic groups are represented.

Cultural/artistic magazines. This category covers all the lively—and not-so-lively arts—music, painting, sculpture, literature, theater, movies and TV. Such magazines can be split into two distinct groups; those directed toward practitioners *(Contemporary Keyboard Magazine, Dramatics Magazine);* and those directed toward patrons and poetasters *(The American Art Journal, Opera Canada).*

Self-improvement magazines. The job of categorizing magazines frequently makes for some mighty strange bedfellows—with this particular category being the winner by five lengths. Self-improvement magazines run the gamut of subjects, including health *(Life and Health);* weight control *(Weight Watchers Magazine);* alternative lifestyles *(Gay Sunshine);* astrology *(Horoscope Guide, Your Personal Astrology);* and making the most of your retirement *(Dynamic Maturity).*

Another subcategory in the self-improvement classification is the religious magazine. Traditionally, educational and inspirational material of interest to a general audience within a specific denomination or religion fits into religious publications. Indeed, many religious magazines are meant to assist lay and professional religious workers in teaching and managing church affairs, while others are striving to help their readers lead better lives. Material published in religious magazines does not have to be strictly religious or inspirational in nature. See *Catholic Digest, Our Family, The National Jewish Monthly,* and *World Encounter.*

Men's magazines. Macho men's adventure magazines such as the now defunct *True* are being replaced by magazines such as *Playboy* and *Penthouse.* The editorial content of some of the other popular men's magazines, notably *Screw* and *Hustler* should possibly be viewed through a keyhole rather than read.

Women's magazines. Magazines for women, whether their slants are feminist or family-oriented, are multiplying by leaps and bounds. They include the confessions *(True Story, Personal Romances);* feminist *(Women: A Journal of Liberation);* special interest *(Bride's Magazine);* family oriented *(Family Circle Magazine);* fashion and self-improvement *(Vogue);* business related *(National Business Woman, Working Woman);* and general interest *(Redbook, McCall's).*

Teen & young adult magazines. Edited for the 13 to 22-year-old audience whose level of sophistication has risen spectacularly in the past decade or two, these magazines now approach the myriad problems that face young people with considerable candor. Most are looking for stories dealing with problems of contemporary teenagers, on such subjects as friendship, dating, family, social prejudice and finding identity. Popular teen magazines include *American Girl* and *Co-ed.*

Juvenile magazines. Toddlers and tads haven't changed much over the years and neither have the publications directed toward the two to 12-year-old set. With many juvenile magazines being published by religious groups, the great mass of publications can be further broken down into smaller-age groups, including children ages two to five, six to eight, and nine to 12. Popular juvenile magazines include *Cricket, Highlights for Children,* and *Wee Wisdom.*

Literary & little magazines. Magazines in this category offer a forum for minority and "far-out" opinions, but don't offer much in the way of payment; most pay in contributor's copies only. They do serve an important purpose, however, since some publish types of material that more commercial magazines wouldn't touch with a ten-foot pole.

Literary magazines, usually sponsored by a college or university, deal mainly in fiction, poetry, and literary criticism. While they are usually more reliable than the "littles" which change addresses often and sometimes don't report on submissions, they are also slow in their reporting times.

Better known literary and little magazines include *Antioch Review, Samisdat, Ball State University Forum, Prairie Schooner, Moons and Lion Tailes, Pigiron, Sewanee Review,* and *The Smith.*

Trade journals. Three types of publications can be accurately fitted into this group of more than 6,000 journals: magazines whose audience is basically composed of retailers; magazines whose audience consists of manufacturers; and those with an audience of professionals, executives and experts. The editorial objective of this first group is to assist readers in making more sales, thus increasing profits. For the manufacturer audience, the thrust is to show them how to more efficiently produce their products. The professionals, executives and experts are shown how they can do their jobs better.

Company/union/association magazine. Gebbie's *House Magazine Directory* lists more than 3,500 "house organs" belonging to companies, clubs, government agencies, and other groups throughout the United States and Canada. Traditionally, house magazines all have some sort of axe or hatchet to grind; frankly promoting the interest of the sponsor is their purpose. Issued on a regular basis, they don't usually carry advertising and are sent free to readers.

Educational Magazines. Many of the educational magazines don't pay, but they're necessary to instructors/professors in publish or perish limbo in United States colleges and universities. Some are general in nature *(Edcentric Magazine)* while others limit their subject matter to a certain field of study *(Day Care and Early Education).*

Miscellaneous magazines. In every field of human endeavor there are always a few "offballs" that can't be categorized. In this catch-all category repose puzzle magazines *(Original Crossword);* magazines geared to special interest groups *(American Atheist Magazine);* and others.

With six different types of articles and 16,000 magazines waiting to gobble them up, it is inconceivable that you can dredge up a subject that isn't salable in article form. Stated another way, your subject can range from aardvarks to zymurgy and, if it is well written, some editor will buy it.

3. Story Ideas — System, Serendipity or Sweat?

William Faulkner once said that all works of literature arise from a passion and an agony of the heart. As a magazine writer, you'll undoubtedly find truth in Faulkner's statement—especially the part about agony, for no writer can avoid writer's block forever. At least once, you'll sit down to stare at your typewriter keys, *sans* ideas.

What to do? "The writer has three sources," Faulkner said. "One is observation; one is experience, which includes reading; the other is imagination, and the Lord only knows where that comes from."

Finding Something to Write About

Whether your ideas come from the front page of the evening *Gazette,* neighborhood gossip, or those weird dreams you have every time you eat green olives and tapioca pudding immediately before going to bed, you should remember one important rule: wherever you go, even if it's only to the john, always carry a pencil and notepad with you. You can never tell when and where a story idea will hit. When it does, jot it down immediately. Story ideas that aren't written down have a strange way of evaporating. The writer will frequently remember he had a story idea, but he won't remember what that idea was.

Most writers use several or all of the following methods in their never-ending search for salable article ideas:

Observation. Nonwriters have the bad habit of being almost totally unobservant; aside from the car in front of them, the TV screen or an attractive member of the opposite sex, they suffer from continual myopia. Writers, however, carefully observe everything around them, looking for something that makes them ask: What? How? Why? These questions usually lead directly to a story idea and, indeed, the answer forms the basis of the resulting article.

Listening. Listening to someone is surely one of the world's easiest occupations unless, of course, it's your mother-in-law. Whenever someone prefaces a question with *what, how* or *why* it should set off the story-idea signal in your brain. This person has acted as an observer for you—the writer—but you are the one who must get busy and evaluate that signal. If the question is of interest only to the person asking the question, or to a very few people, then obviously it doesn't have much merit. If the question has a local angle and is of interest to many people, it will probably work in the local Sunday supplement or a regional magazine. Finally, if it's a question of interest to a broad mass of people, it has the makings of a national story.

Stories from stories. Virtually all writers are insatiable, voracious, omnivorous readers. Through their reading, they are expanding their knowledge so they will be able to write more authoritatively on a broader range of subjects. At the same time, they're finding story ideas. (A fringe benefit of this reading is that they are also improving their techniques through the study of the wordsmithing of other writers.)

A sage once said, "Writing feeds on writing." If ever there was a truism, this is one, because probably more stories evolve from what writers read than from any other single source.

By far, the easiest method of cobbling up a salable story from another story is by furnishing the *why and how* to a story that previously gave only the *who, what, when* and *where*. A writer, by doing this, is developing an interpretive/investigative story from a news story.

Another favored technique is the "opposite stance" method. Here, a writer reads several stories that come to exactly the same conclusion and then writes a story that comes to an opposite conclusion. If the story contains a basis of fact, is well written and well reasoned, it will sell like the proverbial hot cakes. Some writers literally make a fulltime living pounding out these iconoclastic pieces and in the process have come out against just about everything, including babies, Mother's Day and old-age pensions. H.L. Mencken made his literary reputation with this approach and writers such as Nicholas von Hoffman still make a fine living with it.

In their reading, writers also look for the first faint whisper of a fad or trend, since spotting one early can be a real bonanza.

Peter Benchley's book, *Jaws,* literally infected the nation with shark mania. Shark stories proliferated and for awhile, at least, the reading public couldn't learn enough about these demons of the deep.

Similarly, recent attempts to confirm the existence of the Loch Ness Monster have spawned a torrent of other monster stories about the Abominable Snowman, Big Foot, The Jersey Devil and a host of local minimonsters. Tennis has been around since French kings were having their cake and eating it, too, but suddenly, in the early '70s, the sport gained almost overnight popularity. Writers who got in on the ground floor have made a mint writing about everything from home tennis court construction to the psychological aspects of playing mixed doubles.

Even news stories that apparently cover an event or happening in the most minute and redundant detail open up countless avenues for the wide-awake writer. Take the plethora of stories that appeared during the winter of 1976-77 chronicling one of the nation's coldest cold spells. To the uninitiated it would appear that everything that could be written about cold weather was written during this frigid period, but actually, it was only the tip of the iceberg that appeared in print. For years to come, readers will be reading stories similar to "Why utility rates will keep going up," from the February 1977 issue of *Changing Times;* "The Long Winter," from the winter 1975 issue of *Petroleum Today;* and "Winterizing Your Existing Home," from the winter 1976 issue of *Tennessee Valley Perspective.*

Once writers climb aboard a hot subject, they'll ride it right into the ground. The trick, of course, is to climb aboard the subject while it's still fresh.

A news item reported in a newspaper will frequently trigger another type of story called the historical analogy piece. Usually easy to research and write, it concerns a current happening that has a historical counterpart. The writer uses the present situation as his starting point, then describes its historical counterpart in detail, paying particular attention to cause and effect. The writer will often use the historical event to reinforce his conclusion about the current event.

Frequently, a single incident will trigger a rash of historical analogy stories. When it appeared that President Nixon's impeachment was imminent, dozens of writers rushed off to their history books. The historical analogy they came up with was the almost-forgotten impeachment proceedings against Andrew Johnson, 17th president. Even though the analogy between Nixon and Johnson was thin, it became the substance for a hundred-odd stories of this type.

Besides the obvious news story sources, advertisements can also be springboards for articles—especially those ads for offbeat products and services. The following portions of ads offer numerous article possibilities to the writer willing to follow up on them:

LEARN TEN LANGUAGES A YEAR while striding for exercise.

$1,900,000 PROFIT in 30 days guaranteed!

SATANIC CHURCH offering fellowship certificates to hedonistic persons.

ROB BANKS LEGALLY. $2.95.

JOBLESS, FURNITURE STOLEN. Mother of four needs help. God bless you.

You'll find there are sometimes more story ideas lurking in the classified section of a magazine or newspaper than there are on the front page.

The beat. Much like newspaper reporters, professional freelancers develop a "beat." Over the years they learn that some people have an unusual capacity for handing them story ideas. These sources can be judges, criminals, doctors, lawyers, police officers, politicians, educators, businessmen or stockbrokers. No matter who it is, if you discover one of these sources, you would be well advised to not only stay in regular touch with him, but to cherish him. In addition to furnishing you with story ideas, such sources can be helpful in providing informants and information. A writer with a string of sources can often cut his research time in half. Incidentally, some writers are far more prolific than others simply because they have an excellent string of sources.

Gossip. Gossip is to writing what smoke is to fire; both should be investigated!

Almost invariably, there is a basis for gossip even if it's only vindictiveness. Tracking it down may sound like a futile activity, but if the writer is selective about the gossip he spends his time sleuthing, the end result will almost always be a story. Even when the gossip trail peters out, creative writers can still manufacture stories from their raw material, with titles like, "Star Denies Divorce Rumors" and "Beatles Will Not Reunite."

Frequently, a shred of gossip will lead to a real story. The late James Fusca was one of the nation's best, if not most disciplined, investigative writers during the 1960s. His forte was the massive defense and space programs. Stories Jim wrote during this period still have the Department of Defense and NASA beating their breasts and gnashing their teeth whenever they are mentioned. And at least 100 working writers would dearly love to know where and how Jim got his story ideas. Strangely enough, he got them from many of these writers themselves.

Jim was in the habit of spending long hours in the favored haunts of writers. In New York it was Bleeck's, Costello's or the old Overseas Press Club; in Washington it was the National Press Club. His *modus operandi* was always the same. Each evening, as the sun sank into the west, Jim would repair to one of the aforementioned watering holes, anchor his tank-like frame to the bar and listen. Sooner or later one of the habitues would lay a piece of gossip on Jim concerning a glitch in a weapons program, the extramarital lovelife of an astronaut, or whatever. Jim would enter the items in his dog-earred little notebook, take an appreciative sip of Scotch and buy his informant a drink.

While writers truly love to gossip, only about one in 100 will take the time, trouble and expense to track it down. Jim was one of them. When he was the recipient of a bit of intelligence that assayed out to his rather strict specifications he'd be off and running. Watching Jim build his story was like watching a mason build a brick wall. Each hard-earned piece of information that went into the piece was a brick and he built his walls solidly. To get his bricks, he'd poke, pry, puzzle, ponder, pander, push, pull and pout. Somehow, he always got what he was looking for, though it would often take months from the time he first gathered his gossamer of gossip until he completed the piece.

Jim's fall from many editors' grace, by the way, came about because he got too good at his craft. Simply stated, he reached the point where the stories he was ferreting out were too explosive for editors of that era to handle.

Celebrities and characters. Celebrities are seldom born; they're made—by writers. As mentioned previously, people would rather read about people than anything else. More importantly, they're not always particular about the people they read about.

If you think this is an extreme statement, think for a moment about the number of notable people you can name who have never done a single notable thing in their lives. They've achieved their prominence mainly through publicity. They may give parties; they may be well dressed; they may be married or related to men or women of extreme wealth, power or intelligence; they may have been a partner in a highly publicized divorce or adultery. They do, however, share one thing in common. They continually consort with other highly publicized people.

This particular group of celebrities has been tagged with any number of names—society, high society, the international set, the jet set, and most recently, the beautiful people. Although the name of this group changes, its antics and activities do not and many writers make handsome livings playing Boswell to these people.

Doers, achievers, the shakers, the movers, and the king makers make up the second type of celebrity that furnish writers plentiful grist for their typewriters. These are the newsmakers in their specific fields of endeavor—politics, science, the arts, sports, the military. It's not only what these people do that makes stories; it's also what they think.

Finally, we come to those people who occupy the lowest rung on the celebrity ladder—the local character. There's probably no area in the country, no matter how remote, where there aren't several of them running loose about the countryside.

The local character is best defined as some person who has gained a measure of local fame or notoriety for how he acts, something he's done, is doing, or is going to do. Reasons why this person is locally famous can be varied. For example, here are some I've turned up in my home state of Vermont: A gentleman of 85 got married for the third time. Not much of a story here you say? Well, it so happened the bride was 17 and pregnant! Or how about the mother of 13 kids who adopted the 14th because she was superstitious? Or how about the gal who got hitched to a guy who'd been convicted of murdering two previous wives?

Time was when you couldn't give away this type of story, but today there are national magazines that will snap them up faster than you can write them.

The "what if" approach. During World War II, when I was serving as an officer in the Canadian Army, I had a remarkable roommate named William Rose. Bill, who hailed from Jefferson City, Missouri, was a talented guy. He had started out as an artist but sometime during the war decided he was going to earn his living as a writer.

His favorite pastime was lying on his bunk spinning stories, always prefaced with the words "what if."

"What if we were sent to Costa Rica as military attachés?"

"What if we were both awarded the Victoria Cross by mistake?"

Using questions such as these, Bill would skein out a scenario that would leave me with a sore stomach from laughing.

After the war, Bill became a screen writer and has churned out dozens of scripts. Some of his better known offerings are *Flim Flam Man, Genevieve, The Russians Are Coming! The Russians Are Coming!* and *Guess Who's Coming to Dinner?*

If you've seen any of these flicks, you'll quickly perceive that the "what if" technique was used in every single one of them. For years I've know that Bill used this technique in his film writing but, for some strange reason, I didn't think it could be applied to nonfiction magazine writing. I was wrong! In the past few years I've seen literally dozens of articles that have been triggered by the writer asking himself "What if . . . ?"

Subjects are generally problems that could face us in the near future—such as the oil-producing nations jacking prices astronomically, the explosion of a nuclear power plant, or the country suffering through three or four chilling winters in succession. Invariably, the writer uses the "what if" to hypothetically intensify the potential problem, with the resulting article a forecast of what can or may happen. In many cases, the writer will attempt to present a solution.

TV and radio. Viewing TV or listening to the radio can, from time to time, generate a story idea. Most writers, however, view both as secondary sources at best. At worst, they can be exceedingly counterproductive to a writer who doesn't need much of an excuse to goof off!

Personal experience. Most beginning writers are obsessed with writing about themselves, probably because they have a difficult time getting ideas about anything else.

The problem with writing about yourself is that editors and readers aren't really interested in reading about you, unless your story fits one of the following criteria:

You've overcome a problem that faces a large number of people and these people can solve or minimize their problem by reading your story.

From experience, you know how to do something better, easier or cheaper than anyone else and in your story, you tell readers how they can do it.

You've had an experience or adventure so unique, exciting or humorous that thousands of people will read about it for sheer entertainment.

If your personal experience story doesn't fit one of these slots, you'd be well advised to forget it. If you don't, you're only going to be wasting time and paper.

Writer at Work

To understand how a working writer employs these story-generating techniques, let's follow a not-so-fictional pro around for a day. We'll call him Vladimir Nimbus. Vlad, who served his apprenticeship as a newspaper reporter and magazine editor, has been a fulltime freelancer for 15 years and is known in the trade as a generalist writer. In other words, he'll aim his typewriter at any target of opportunity as long as the price is right.

He makes his home, when he's not on assignment, in Cherry Hill, New Jersey, and for good reason. It allows him to work in a semirural environment, yet New York City with all its magazine editors is just 90 bus minutes away. Equally important, in event of a hurry-up assignment, Vlad can get to the Philadelphia Municipal Airport in 21 minutes.

The day we've picked to shadow Vlad is not really a typical one. Today, he will journey to the city to deliver a manuscript and discuss two assignments with editors.

At 5:30 his hausfrau boots him out of bed and tells him it's time to get marching. Vlad stumbles into the shower and finally wakes up. Most days, when he's working at his typewriter, he foregoes shaving. Today, he shaves. As he splashes on some new aftershave lotion his wife bought him for his birthday he notices something strange. The lotion not only smells better than the brand he was using, but the small amount that has hit his lips tastes better. This rings a bell. The other week when he kissed his wife he noticed her lipstick had a faint fruit flavor. He goes to the bedroom, grabs his notepad from the night table and jots down the following: *Are cosmetic companies making their products taste better? Check public relations departments of Revlon, Faberge and Estee Lauder. Possibility for short for women's or men's mags.*

The smell of frying bacon attracts Vlad to the kitchen. As he sits down, his wife puts a bowl of strawberries and a container of Cool Whip in front of him.

"Where's the whipped cream for the berries?" he asks.

"Right in front of you, darling!"

"That stuff isn't whipped cream."

"Well, the TV commercials say it tastes better than whipped cream and besides it's cheaper; so eat!"

Vlad's response is a four-letter word of Anglo-Saxon origin. Gingerly, he picks up the container of Cool Whip and reads the label: "Ingredients: water, hydrogenated coconut and palm kernel oils, sugar, corn syrup solids, sodium caseinate, dextrose, polysorbate 60, natural and artificial flavors, sorbitan monostearate, carrageenan, guar gum and artificial color."

He puts down the container of Cool Whip, sprinkles his strawberries with sugar, fishes his notepad and pencil from his shirt pocket and makes this cryptic entry: *Cool Whip label. Do piece on nonfood foods. Title: "Future Farmers of America: The Chemists."* Reader's Digest *maybe.*

When Vlad gets to the bus station he buys a copy of *The Wall Street Journal* and watches the long line of regular commuters with bemused sympathy. Every one of them is carrying an attache case. They obviously belong to a group that *Fortune* is in the habit of calling middle management.

When he boards the bus, he sits well to the rear. This gives him the advantage of being able to see everything that goes on. As the bus heads up the New Jersey Turnpike toward the Big Apple, a curious thing happens. Within minutes, newspapers begin to flutter to the aisle and the commuters begin dozing off. By the time the bus has passed the Bordentown exit, 90% of the passengers are asleep. The other ten percent is staring vacantly out the window. Not one passenger has opened his attache case.

Vlad figures that each person on the bus spends a minimum of 20 hours a week commuting to and from a 35-hour-a-week job. In other words they are spending almost one-seventh of their working lives in the nonproductive pursuit of commuting. Could it be made more productive? He remembers how a friend of his, the late Bob Colburn, who was assistant managing editor of *Business Week,* once wrote a book while commuting between Connecticut and New York City. Out comes the notepad. *Do story on commuting. Slant it toward making it more productive. Use actual examples like Bob C. Check markets.*

Vlad next turns to his copy of *The Wall Street Journal.* It's Monday and there's not much in it that he hasn't already read in the Sunday *New York Times.* Finally, his eye falls on a small advertisement that offers "graduate college degrees with no academic work." The ad carries a New Jersey address.

What do readers of *The Wall Street Journal* need phony college degrees for? Vlad muses a minute or two, then writes the address in his notepad and adds the following: *Piece on phony job qualifications? Check personnel departments of major corporations. Follow up on ad. May be good shot for* Esquire.

The bus speeds north and the rotten egg smell of mercaptan gives Vlad the olfactory news that they are approaching Elizabeth and Newark, one of the nation's most heavily-industrialized areas. He watches with interest as they pass mazes of oil refineries, tank farms, power plants, dock facilities and chemical plants. In a small creek that flows through one of the largest tank farms, there's a flock of more than 100 mallards paddling happily about. As the bus comes abreast of the huge Newark Airport, Vlad sees 18 or 20 pheasants pecking diligently in the sere grass at the end of a runway. A 747 lumbers noisily skyward above the unperturbed pheasants.

A few miles north, the bus swings past the Jersey Swamps and over the Hackensack River. In a setback close to the Turnpike are hundreds of ducks, egrets by the dozens and several sentinel-like blue herons. The placid surface of the setback is dotted by mound-like muskrat houses. In the distance is the New York City skyline.

Vlad grabs his notepad and writes, *More wildlife (birds), etc. to be seen in N.J. around oil refineries (Elizabeth and Newark) than at some wildlife refuges. Why? Are some species adapting to polluted environment? Check* American Museum of Natural History. *Would make good article for* Smithsonian *or* National Geographic. *Spin-off piece: If there are thousands of muskrats in the Jersey Swamps, somebody must be trapping them. Check bridge keeper of drawbridge over Hackensack River and find out who trappers are. Great story for* New York Magazine. *Title: Was Your Fur Coat Trapped Five Miles From Manhattan?*

In New York, Vlad hops a crosstown bus and, because he's early for his first appointment, decides to walk up Lexington Avenue. As he passes an umbrella store his attention is caught by the window display. There are not many umbrellas in it, but there are whips of every variety, including a deadly looking cat-o-nine-tails. Out comes the notepad and into it goes the following notation: *Is the growing interest in SM revitalizing the nation's buggy whip industry? Check retail outlets and whip manufacturers. Could be humorous piece for* Playboy *or* Penthouse.

Less than half a block away Vlad looks up and, though he's walked Lexington Avenue hundreds of times, sees something he has never noticed before. The portico overhanging Grand Central Terminal is held in place by four simulated hawsepipes that secure ships to a dock. Each is equipped with a funnel-like device used to prevent rats from boarding vessels while in port. In the case of the Grand Central hawsepipes, however, there's a fat bronze rat climbing up each of them. Vlad smiles. It's obvious the architect had a sense of humor as well as a feeling for symbology.

Three blocks up Lexington, he looks at the portico over the entrance of the Belmont Hotel. It's held up by the heads of four elephants. Each of the golden pachyderms seems to be smiling. Out comes the notepad and in goes the quick entry, *Grand Central rats. Belmont Hotel elephants. Do story on architectural humor. OK for Sunday* New York Times Magazine.

At his first stop, where he is to discuss an assignment, the editor literally smothers him with praise. Vlad is momentarily taken aback. Praise is something he hasn't received much of from editors.

"Boy, am I ever glad to see you Vlad, baby," the editor gushes. "You're the first responsible writer to walk into this office in months. Sorry I can give you only two weeks to do this job, but like I said on the phone, I'll give you an extra 500 bucks. You're a pro and I know damn well you'll deliver a solid piece we'll both be proud of.

"Under normal circumstances I'd never put you under the gun like this, but Peter Plit really screwed me up on this piece. Gave him the assignment two months ago, but instead of getting his tail behind his typewriter he went off on another binge. He's shacked up out in Southampton with some cupcake that drinks as much as he does and they won't even answer the phone.

"Damn it all, Vlad, what's with writers these days? Present company excluded, of course, it seems they're all lushes. What is it? Does writing drive them to drink or do they drink in order to write?

"Oh, well, why should I burden you with an editor's problems when you've got enough of your own. Anyway, here's the poop on this assignment . . ."

On the way out of the magazine's editorial offices Vlad stops in the reception area long enough to make this entry in his notepad: *Does writing drive writers to drink or do writers drink in order to write? Do serious piece on writers and alcoholism. Hemingway, Faulkner, Fitzgerald, Thomas, Cheever, et al. Possible for* Atlantic.

Vlad picks up another assignment, drops off an article and, after a quick lunch at the Algonquin where he learns that *National Geographic* is making some changes in its editorial format and *New York Magazine* is upping its manuscript rates, he heads for home.

As the bus speeds south he starts to thumb through a copy of *The Village Voice*. On page two there's an ad which Vlad copies in his pad

along with his own comments: *Anything for a price as long as it's legal.
Practical jokes and serious inquiries. 877-9696. If this guy or gal does
anything more than walk dogs it could be a piece for* People *magazine.
Call next time in NY.*

As Vlad drives from the bus terminal in Cherry Hill to his home,
he passes a ski shop where he notices the parking lot is full of cars.
Here it is, the last week in June and customers are literally breaking
down the doors of a store that sells skis. How come? Pulling up in
front of his house, he makes another notation in the notepad. *Check
out ski shop on Route 41 re: high volume business in June. Could be fast
article for* Skiing Trade News."

Vlad gets in three hours behind his typewriter before it's time to
leave for a small dinner party with his wife. During the course of the
evening the talk turns to gambling.

"What effect do you think the new casinos in Atlantic City will
have on gambling in Las Vegas?" one guest asks.

"Ha," another replies, "it'll kill 'em! But it won't be just Atlantic
City. Before you know it Pennsylvania will pass a law allowing gambling in the Poconos. New York will see the revenues it's losing and
get casinos approved for the Catskills. Then Miami Beach will get
into the act and before you know it every resort area in the country—
even the ski areas in Vermont and Colorado—will have gambling.
Hell, look what's happening to state lotteries!"

Vlad moves off into a corner and makes the following entry in his
pad: *Gambling! The Nation's Newest Growth Industry. Start doing
research on economic, sociological and psychological impact of gambling.* Harper's?

That night, the last thing Vlad does is put his notepad on the night
table beside his bed. As he does so he turns the small yellow stub of a
pencil over in his hand. He smiles and makes one last entry: *How are
conventional pencil manufacturers doing these days in face of competition from ball- and felt-point writing instruments? Could make good story for* Signature Magazine. *Check manufacturers. Also find out what is
the most expensive writing instrument sold. Could be wrap-up type
article.*

Amazing? Not really. Vlad got only 13 story ideas, which is probably an average daily figure for most pros. But his story ideas, you'll notice, give him a big advantage. Most of them are not perishable; he can write the stories when he gets around to it. The biggest problem he has is for another writer to stumble onto one of his ideas and sell it first. This happens so rarely, though, that most writers seldom worry about it.

4. The Query

I get livid when I read in a book or magazine article that the query is a panacea for all beginning writers. Supposedly, the query will save them from wasting their time researching and writing a story that isn't marketable. Tripe! The one thing that will save a beginning writer a lot of time is to *stop writing queries and write articles.*

In theory the prime purpose of the so-called editorial query is to sell the editor on your article before you write it. In practice, it doesn't always accomplish this end. For example, there are times when an editor should never be queried. Here are some of them:

You're a beginning writer and have sold only a few articles. The only thing your query proves is that you can write a query; it doesn't prove you can write a publishable 2,500-word article. Beginning writers must prove themselves by furnishing editors with completed manuscripts.

You've picked a magazine that pays less than $150. Most of these smaller markets want manuscripts, not queries.

You're contemplating doing a short piece of 1,000-1,500 words for a Sunday supplement or magazine. You figure it will take you almost as long to write a meaningful query as to complete the article.

You're considering doing a piece, but when you try to do a query that conveys any coherent meaning to the editor you find the task impossible. Humorous pieces, you'll find, will invariably fall into this category.

By now you're wondering if you should ever send a query. The answer, of course, is yes, but it is a qualified yes. First, you should evaluate the types of queries you can use, then decide the best approach for each of your article projects. You may find that it is best to query for certain types of articles, while for others, it is to your advantage to submit the finished piece.

Types of Queries

Writers often use the article outline query—a dull, deadly, murderous instrument that will result in a high proportion of turndowns. The only time this type of query should be used is when it is sent to an editor who is familiar with your work.

When you do send one, don't use the standard outline form you learned in school. Instead, summarize the article in terse language and use a logical sequence—beginning, middle, end. Include information on photos and length of time it will take you to complete the article.

A better approach to querying is the query letter, which at its best is a letter that nobody—not even an editor—can put down. In it, you'll want to hit him hard and fast with the story idea you have in mind, using facts, figures, provocative statements, and even questions to whet his interest. Make sure the letter is specific. You might want to briefly quote someone who will be interviewed in the article.

Don't tell the entire story in the query, though. Use just enough ammo to catch the editor's interest; make him want to hear the rest of the story and you've got a sale.

Art Spikol, executive editor of *Philadelphia* magazine, received a query from a woman who told him about the possibly thousands of people who had "time bombs" in their throats. They had been treated, as children, with X-rays that were meant to inhibit growth of tonsils, but those X-rays might instead be related to throat cancer today. Unfortunately, the author said, these people don't know they had the X-ray treatments and/or that those treatments may be linked to cancer.

Says Spikol: If she didn't have me then, she threw in the clincher: did I care what happened to her when a growth was found in her own throat, a growth thought to have been caused by that kind of X-ray therapy? Sure I did. In fact, I started worrying about my own throat. She got the assignment.

Granted, the above-mentioned author had some pretty dramatic stuff in her query. But, all the same, she followed the rules. First, grab the editor's attention right in the first sentence. He might receive a hundred queries per day and to sell your article, you'll have to make him set up and take notice. Then, pull him down into the meat of the story right away, giving him a firm idea of what the article will be about *without* telling him the entire story from beginning to end.

The query's last graph should list your recent writing credits. If your work is not known to the editor, it might also help to include a couple tearsheets, to give him an idea of your writing style and also to prove to him that you *can* write. If the letter runs more than a page and a half, you're in trouble, so start over and keep it short—one page, preferably.

Sound easy? Don't kid yourself. Many talented writers find it harder to write a hard-hitting query that will sell an editor than to write the article itself. If you find you suffer from this problem—and it's no disgrace—there is another alternative: Write three pages of the article and on the fourth page outline the remainder, paying particular attention to its conclusion. Send this to the editor with a brief cover letter listing your published pieces. If you have a salable article, this type of query will bring fast and positive results because, first of all, it demonstrates to the editor that you can write. Secondly, it gives him a clear, concise idea of what your article is about. Finally, it gives him the opportunity to make an editorial judgment based on something other than circumstantial evidence.

The final way of querying an editor is by calling him. A word of caution, though: use this approach only if you know the editor or if you stumble onto a story that is so perishable you can't go through normal channels. Editors work hard for a living, are faced with constant deadlines and don't have time for idle chit-chat with even their most prized authors. So, if you want to become one of those prized authors, don't call unless it's absolutely necessary.

The Waiting Game

After writing a query, "money" writers usually send it to more than one editor. By doing this, they are, in effect, holding an auction by mail to see which editor will pay the most for the piece. Remember, there is nothing dishonest about sending multiple inquiries as long as you play fair and advise them you are also offering the piece to several other editors simultaneously. If you don't advise them and subsequently get more than one offer for your piece, you had better be prepared to write the editors you are turning down a letter that would make a diplomat proud. After all, you don't want to be blacklisted at a particular market because the editor, who invested time and interest in your article idea, had to be told the piece he planned to buy had been sold elsewhere.

After the query is sent, you'll probably spend considerable time hovering near your mailbox awaiting the bad or (hopefully) good news. It usually comes in one of four forms:

The editor gives you a flat, but usually friendly "No!"

The editor is interested in your piece, but his constricted editorial budget precludes him from making you an offer at this time. He requests that you do the article on speculation ("spec") and he'll give you a decision when he sees the finished product.

The editor loves your piece and gives you the go-ahead but, there's a catch. He'll pay you a $50 "kill fee" if he doesn't use the article and $350 if he does. This is a common practice extended by editors usually only to writers whose work is familiar to them. Pros have learned by bitter experience that kill fees don't buy many groceries.

The editor is ecstatic about your story idea. He'll buy it! Better yet he'll pay you an immediate advance plus a generous check for your expenses!

If you're a beginning writer, the answers to your queries will likely fall into the first three categories. The last category is reserved for battle-scarred journeymen with 100 or more published stories under their belts. But, be of good cheer. If you keep plugging away, you may not have to worry about querying editors. When, and if, you get really good, they'll start querying you.

5. Seek and Ye Shall Find —You Hope!

The history and folklore of writing is replete with accounts (both real and imagined) of research efforts that make Stanley's quest for Livingstone look like a Sunday outing. Truman Capote, for example, spent five years putting together the mosaic that became *In Cold Blood*. *Roots* required 12 years of dogged and expensive research by Alex Haley.

Of course, these epic efforts had happy endings. Both authors became millionaires. But what about authors of magazine articles? Research can literally make or break the budding magazine writer. The reason, of course, is pure economics.

Unless you've discovered a way to eat bylines, it doesn't make much sense to spend 40 hours researching and ten hours writing an article for which you'll be paid only $40. So, how much research should you do? The answer is: *As little as possible!*

Now, hold on a bit. I'm not advocating you slough off in the research department nor am I espousing the cause of passing fiction off as fact. What I am saying is that you must be careful, very careful, in equating time spent with benefits (in the case of most writers it's money) received. Writers are no different than other professionals—doctors, dentists, lawyers, accountants. The clock on the wall can be, and often is, your biggest enemy.

Before you start work on *any* research article try to figure out where your research sources are, how much time it will take to mine them, and the expenses, if any, involved. Obviously, you'll come up with only the roughest of approximations but, at least, you'll have a guesstimate of what's involved and whether the pig is worth the poke.

Unless an article is a first person piece, editors have no way of knowing whether it is of the nonresearch variety. I've asked several editors how many nonresearch pieces run in national magazines and all think the figure is around five percent. I've posed this same question to a dozen writers and most of them have just given me a grunt or a shrug. The few who have made a guess think it's *less* than five percent. Drawing on my own experience, I've sold only 15 to 20 articles of this type in 25 years. Thus, it seems highly unlikely that any writer, no matter how talented, could make a living sticking solely to this easy-to-do genre.

Incidentally, some magazine articles are highly deceptive. While superficially, they appear to be nonresearch pieces, the author may have actually spent long hours in the library researching facts that he already had in hand.

Some magazines are sticklers for accuracy, so your choice of a market may have much to do with the amount of time you spend researching your story. Off the top of my head, I can guarantee you that a sloppy or incomplete research job won't ever slip by the editors of *Reader's Digest, The New Yorker* or *National Geographic*. Naturally, all reputable national magazines demand accuracy but this trio represents the toughest of the tough. Let me give you a single example of how magazines of this caliber go about researching a writer's research.

A number of years ago a friend of mine, Bill Coughlin, wrote a piece for *Reader's Digest* that concerned the first man to successfully bail out of an airplane traveling at supersonic speed. In order to get his story, Bill interviewed the guy at length. During the course of the interview, the subject, a civilian test pilot who had been flying an F-100, told Bill he'd been wearing a brown sweater the day he'd hit the silk.

A short time after *Reader's Digest* had gotten the story, the magazine queried Bill about the color of the sweater. Bill dutifully called the pilot to check. Wonder of wonders, on reflection the pilot recalled he'd been wearing a blue sweater on the day of the accident. By this time, Bill was beginning to think the magazine was using mental telepathy to second-guess his research. As it turned out, the occult had nothing to do with it. Seems a researcher from *Reader's Digest,* in checking out the story, had talked with the captain of the fishing boat that had plucked the pilot from San Francisco Bay and the captain had mentioned that the pilot had been wearing a *blue* sweater.

Using Your Head

Frequently, you may have to travel several thousand miles for a single story. If you're smart you'll try to get several stories for the price of your airline ticket—even if the ticket is free. Some years back, the West German government invited 18 of us writers to tour the country. Insofar as the party was composed of some pretty famous names, I figured I would learn plenty from my distinguished colleagues. Unfortunately, during the two weeks we spent traveling about the German countryside, the only thing I learned was that most of them could drink more than I could. There was, however, a lone lady in the party—Frances Koltun, then travel editor of *Glamour* magazine—from whom I learned a lesson about the importance of preliminary research.

Frances, prior to leaving New York, had spent plenty of time doing her homework. She'd studied our itinerary carefully and knew exactly what she wanted to see and who she wanted to interview. While the rest of us were slopping down the products of Rhine vineyards, she was addressing intelligent questions to the winegrower. If we were eating, she'd be in the restaurant's kitchen getting the chef's prize recipe. While the rest of us were lounging at a sunny sidewalk cafe, she'd be racing off to visit some nearby cathedral.

I never found out how many articles this hard-working gal dredged up from this single trip, but I'd be willing to wager a considerable amount that it was more than all the rest of us combined. Over the years Frances has written many travel books and hundreds of articles, and has appeared regularly on the *Today* show. In the process, she has become one of the best and most authoritative travel writers in the country.

The moral of this story is that you should economize by researching several articles simultaneously. If you have to travel to a large university library miles away from your home base, you'll save both time and money by working on as many as four or five articles during your library visit even if you don't plan to start writing these articles for another few weeks. Before you journey to the library, plan your research carefully so that you know exactly what you're looking for. That way you'll get everything in one fell swoop. There's not much profit in making a long trip to the library, only to return home and find you've forgotten to search out a critical point.

Standard Reference Books

Before you embark on any long and possibly unproductive research projects, try to find what you are looking for in what librarians refer to as "standard" or "basic" reference books. In most libraries these are located in one general area, with tables nearby where you can jot down your findings in comfort, if not always quiet. (With respect to the latter, most seasoned writers try to get their library work done before the local high school lets out.)

There are literally thousands of standard reference books on the shelves. Consequently, we'll confine this brief listing to those most helpful to the magazine writer. We'll start with reference books about reference books.

Guide to Reference Books and *Subject Guide to Reference Books.* The first volume lists all manner of specialized encyclopedias and other sources, while the other will give you a rundown on what's available according to subject. Both books can be big time-savers.

Oxford English Dictionary. This 13-volume work is frequently referred to as the *OED* or *NED* (New English Dictionary) by scholars and librarians. It is considered to be the most authoritative and complete English dictionary available, and contains 414,825 words. This supposedly is *every* English word in use up to the time of its publication. Unfortunately, it does not contain obscene words, which is rather a pity in view of recent publishing trends. Of particular interest to the writer is the fact that the *OED* contains 1,827,306 quotations, which is far more than *Bartlett's Familiar Quotations,* Stevenson's *Home Book of Quotations,* Mencken's *New Dictionary of Quotations on Historical Principles from Ancient & Modern Sources,* or Smith's *Oxford Dictionary of English Proverbs.*

Roget's International Thesaurus (1962). The standard compilation of synonyms arranged under subject categories which are cross referenced. The failure of this book is that it does not distinguish between words of like meaning. Because of this, many writers use it in conjunction with *Webster's Dictionary of Synonyms* which carefully distinguishes between words of like meaning and lists antonyms as well.

Slang And Its Analogues, by J.S. Farmer and W.E. Henley. While there are several excellent slang dictionaries available, this one is the most comprehensive. It lists more than 100,000 words with their meanings and derivations together with illustrative quotations and synonyms in French, German, Italian and Spanish.

Biographical Indexes. Writers, it seems, are continually tracking down people and information about them. If the person in question is not a full-blown public figure or an important historical figure, this can be a time-consuming effort. The first thing that must be established in using *Biographical Indexes* is whether the person is among the quick or the dead. If he's written a book or had a book written about him, check the card catalog in your local library. Years of birth and death are usually listed. Failing this, you may have to check several different sources. If you suspect that the individual has left this orb, you'd be well advised to check the *Dictionary of Biography.* Should your subject be of British origin, your best bet is the *Dictionary of National Biography.* Both works will also furnish you with excellent bibliographic material. Other sources where it may be possible to locate biographical material on deceased individuals include *National Cyclopaedia of American Biography, Appleton's Cyclopaedia of American Biography* (1887-1900), and *Who Was Who in America* (of which there is a British edition).

If the person you're tracking down is still extant rather than extinct, your most authoritative source is either the American or British editions of *Who's Who.* There are also a growing number of biographical dictionaries that are compiled along professional, ethnic and religious lines. Representative ones include *Who's Who in American Education, Who's Who in American Art, Italian-American Who's Who, Who's Who in Colored America, Who's Who in American Jewry* and *American Catholic Who's Who.*

A word of warning: be extremely cautious when using these volumes for research. In many cases the biographies were written by the people themselves and as a consequence, many entries are a bit suspect when it comes to accuracy and/or modesty.

Other reference volumes that will assist you in smoking out international personalities are *International Who's Who, Webster's Biographical Dictionary, Chambers' Biographical Dictionary, Biography Index* and *World Biography.*

Encyclopedias. For many writers, encyclopedias are the most valued of all reference books and should be the point of departure for most research projects. As the name implies, these works are summaries of man's knowledge. The writer, by using them, can gain a fast survey of virtually any subject in easily-digestible form. Equally important, most encyclopedias contain bibliographies on every imaginable subject, so they can provide you with positive indications about the direction your succeeding research should take.

Many writers will invariably consult more than one encyclopedia even though they find the information they're seeking in the first source. Articles in the best encyclopedias are written by leading experts—experts who frequently come to different conclusions. Obviously, the inclusion of two opposing points of view can add considerable interest to the resulting article. Similarly, one encyclopedia may contain titles in its bibliographies that aren't listed in another. If your research project is going to be an extensive one, you will be saving yourself much time and travail by gathering as many sources as possible at the outset.

The writer should be acquainted with the two really outstanding encyclopedias, the most famous of which is the *Encyclopedia Britannica.* In recent years this work has undergone some extensive revisions and a radical change in format. It is available in virtually all libraries and is subject to continuous revision.

Encyclopedia Americana is an excellent source for authors writing about American topics. Its articles have been written by leading scholars and experts, and are signed. Like *Britannica,* this valuable research tool is under constant revision.

For convenience, you'll find the *Columbia Encyclopedia* hard to beat. This single-volume work contains more than 70,000 entries, including a large number of biographical sketches with bibliographies.

If you have a second language capability, you may want to investigate foreign encyclopedias. Regardless of what your second language is, you'll find one or more encyclopedias written in it, but the problem is that these foreign works can be found only in the larger public or university libraries. Another disadvantage is that many of them are badly out-of-date.

Specialized Encyclopedias. Since World War II, there has been an almost explosive proliferation of specialized encyclopedias. Almost every area of scholarship has at least one and, in some of the more popular disciplines, as many as 20.

In addition to specialized encyclopedias, each field of study in the arts, sciences and humanities has a number of indexes and bibliographies. The quickest, indeed perhaps the only, way to find out which ones are best suited for your research is to ask someone who is actively engaged in the field of study in which you're working.

Atlases. These reference books are frequently overlooked by writers, but can often provide valuable information. In addition to locating countries, cities and towns, they can assist you in visualizing geographical locations of events, tracing the voyages of explorers, locating birthplaces, and checking facts that concern rainfall, weather, mineral deposits and population.

Atlases can be either general or historical. The general atlas is a contemporary work providing current boundaries and up-to-date demographic and geographic information. I've often used the *Hammond Medallion World Atlas,* which even contains zip codes. Another excellent general work is *The Times Atlas of the World.*

If your research is moving you back into history, you'd do well to consult the four-volume *Literary and Historical Atlas,* or the *Cambridge Modern Historical Atlas,* which covers the period from 1490 to 1910. If your research concerns the North American continent, you'll likely find what you're looking for in the *Atlas of the Historical Geography of the United States.* This work is particularly valuable because it delineates the development and settlement of the United States and depicts the geographic boundaries at different periods. It also offers the researcher a wealth of information concerning economic development and immigration.

Periodicals and Books

Searching periodicals for information on your chosen subject can be helpful in two important ways: It can be a prime research source and can also indicate whether the subject you intend to tackle has been done before, by whom, and in what manner.

Virtually all libraries contain periodical indexes which list articles appearing in selected periodicals under subject, title and author's name. By using them, you can track down articles in hundreds of magazines, both past and present, that may have a bearing on your subject. At last count there were more than 15 of these indexes. Here are the most important ones:

Reader's Guide to Periodical Literature (1900 to present) is the standard guide to periodical literature. Updated on a monthly basis, it indexes about 140 publications, most of them of a general nature.

If what you are looking for doesn't show up in the *Reader's Guide,* your next best bet is the *International Index to Periodicals* (1907 to present). This index is similar to *Reader's Guide,* except that it also includes many foreign magazines as well as scholarly journals.

If your research involves the 19th century, you'll have to turn to *Poole's Index to Periodical Literature* (1802 to 1906) which covers both British and American periodicals of this period. The shortcoming of this reference work is that it is a subject index with no author or title entries, except for works that can't be categorized under a subject, such as poems and novels.

Union List of Serials is a reference work that can be used profitably in conjunction with the foregoing publications. It lists periodicals available in various American and Canadian libraries. Names of periodicals are followed by a code indicating the name and location of libraries where they can be found.

To make sure you get all the information you need, jot down an outline of what *you think* you are going to need before you step foot inside the library. Obviously, as you get deeper into your research you may find that you'll be going in different directions from what you had originally anticipated. This occurs frequently, but your outline, at least, gives you a path to follow at the outset and keeps you from straying onto time-consuming, nonproductive detours.

Before you begin any research you'll need a supply of 5x8 note cards, which are inexpensive and readily available. When you uncover a research source that contains material for your article, enter the title of the source, author, page number, and where the source was found at the top of the card. Then jot down the material you are extracting. Use a separate card for each source. If you use a notebook during field research, it's a good idea to transcribe this material onto cards before your notes get "cold." By using this technique you'll save much time and trouble.

Now you're ready to begin the perilous peregrination into the realm of research. Where do you begin? This, of course, depends upon the subject matter of the article you are going to write. If you're writing about something that happened yesterday, you're going to utilize different research sources than you'd use if you were writing about something that happened 3,000 years ago. Because of this, let's take a look at the major research sources.

Research Sources

Kitchen research. This is one of the easiest, most comfortable ways of doing research because it can be done in the confines of your own home. As mentioned in a previous chapter, most writers are voracious readers. I know several who read two or three newspapers a day and 40 to 50 magazines each and every month. Their insatiable reading habits broaden their knowledge and help supply them with story ideas.

Let's assume that during your daily reading sessions you see a small item you think may be the seed of a story that is going to germinate and grow into something big. You clip the story, paste it onto one of your 5x8 cards, note the source and date, and file it under the heading you've chosen. If it's a fast-developing story, you may be adding 30 to 40 clippings from newspapers and magazines to your collection each week.

On the other hand, you may be lucky to get only three or four clippings a year. No matter. At some point you'll finally accumulate enough "kitchen research" to sit down and write your story.

Does this type of research pay off? The answer is a resounding, "Yes!" Consider Emalene Shepherd, a successful Cincinnati freelance writer and instructor for the Writer's Digest School, who uses her own brand of "kitchen research" for many of her articles. She describes herself as "a lazy writer who works only a few hours a day at home," yet she has sold to publications such as *American Girl, American Baby, The Christian Mother, The New York Times, Cincinnati, Lookout, Teen Talk, Success Unlimited,* and *The Christian Home.*

How often have you read an interpretive, investigative or roundup story that literally staggered you with the amount of scholarship and research that went into its writing? Scholarship? Research? My foot! A large number of these impressive articles are conjured up by perceptive writers who used the exact, same, simple approach I've described here. If you find this a bit hard to believe then I suggest you read a few of A.J. Liebling's *Wayward Press* articles that appeared in *The New Yorker* or some of Bernard De Voto's *Easy Chair* columns that appeared in *Harper's Magazine*. You'll quickly become a believer even though it's highly unlikely you'll ever become another Leibling or DeVoto! A few words of advice about kitchen research: Try to keep several projects going at one time. The more you have cooking, the more salable stories you'll develop. Normally, I'm clipping for 20 to 30 at the same time. I know several writers who enlist their wives or husbands to assist them in their clipping activities and some of them are clipping for as many as 150 stories at a time. Whatever you do, don't get discouraged if a story doesn't evolve in a few months. Keep on clipping. I've kept at it for years on many topics before my scissorwork paid off. Here's a confession: In my files right now is a story for which the first clip goes back 23 years. I need just one more bit of information before I crank it into my typewriter. I may get this elusive fragment tomorrow or five years from tomorrow, but I'm certain I'm going to get it. There is some consolation in this long wait. It's been my experience that the longer it takes for a story to bloom, the bigger the manuscript check will be. The reason is that your story is likely to be a real "exclusive" and an editor will pay premium rates for it.

From time-to-time you may find yourself clipping for a story that can literally be written in installments; as the story progresses you can keep doing articles on it. The most stories I've been able to get out of a single kitchen research subject was three, but I know of a couple of lucky writers who have managed to milk six manuscript checks out of one growing pile of clippings over a period of a few years.

Newspapers. If your story idea concerns a contemporary event, happening or personality, the "morgue" of your local or area newspaper is a good place to start your research. Don't let the word "morgue" scare you off. This is newspaper parlance for a department where clips, photos, and reference materials are filed for use by the newspaper staff. The quality and extent of these morgues varies markedly from newspaper to newspaper. In the case of weeklies and small city dailies it might be a cubbyhole containing a few dozen file cabinets and the bound volumes of back issues, while big-city dailies usually have elaborate, well-indexed morgues staffed with competent people. A goodly number of these large dailies maintain their "clip files" on microfilm systems that make the retrieval of information fast and relatively painless.

Another advantage you'll find when you use a morgue belonging to a large daily newspaper is that many of them clip from a large number of sources—including other major newspapers, smaller area newspapers, news magazines, and, in a few cases, the *Congressional Record* when entries pertain to the activities of the area's congressional delegation. These larger morgues also contain a vast amount of other materials that may be unavailable even in local and area libraries. Items available might include early city maps, old photos, old school annuals and yearbooks, business directories from the past, and bound volumes of defunct area newspapers and magazines.

You can get permission to use a newspaper morgue by asking the receptionist, who will probably refer you to the head librarian or editor. State your case by telling him or her about the article you have in preparation and the material you hope to find. Invariably, assuming you're not a wild-eyed anarchist, you'll receive permission to use the morgue. In 30 years of writing I've never been turned down, nor have I ever heard of any other *serious* writer who hasn't been successful in gaining access to these important research sources.

There are, however, a few rules of conduct you'd be well-advised to follow if you don't want to wear out your welcome. Always have your research organized. Ask for everything you need at one time. Don't keep requesting new files every half hour or so. Never forget, the newspaper is doing you a favor by allowing you to use their facilities; it's not the other way around.

Don't steal *anything* out of a file, no matter how unimportant it may seem. Don't ask to have an item or items photocopied. If one of the employees volunteers, fine. Otherwise, forget it. Be appreciative. If the people who work in a morgue have been particularly cooperative and helpful, show your appreciation with a box of chocolates or some other small gift. You'll be pleasantly surprised to see how such a simple, inexpensive gesture pays off.

Now, let's assume you've poked through your local morgue and you've struck out. You can't turn up what you're looking for. *Don't give up,* for you may find that elusive bit of information by using one of the following indexes which are available in most large- and medium-sized libraries:

The New York Times Index (1894 to 1904; 1913 to date). An index of news and feature stories that have appeared in this "newspaper of record," it is issued annually and provides the date, page, and column of each entry. Entries are arranged alphabetically by subject and individual. If the subject of your article is biographical, historical, social or political, you'll find this index an indispensable research tool.

The Official Index of The London Times (1906 to date) This index, published annually, is of value to writers researching a subject with a European/British slant. It is also useful in gaining insight into the European viewpoint of an event.

The New York Daily Tribune Index (1875 to 1906). Insofar as this index predates the *New York Times* index by 18 years, it can be an important source for writers whose research leads them into this period.

American Newspapers, 1921-1936, by Winifred Gregory. A listing of newspapers in possession of libraries, state and local historical societies, other organizations and private collections, this volume is an important research source because it can assist the writer in locating the hard-to-find newspaper. It may also save considerable travel expense by listing libraries where the publication is available.

History and Bibliography of American Newspapers, 1690-1820, by Clarence S. Brigham. If your research is carrying you back into American history, you'll find this is an invaluable guide. It lists, by town and state, the newspapers published during this period and where copies repose today. This volume also contains historical information about the founding, publishers, and editors of these newspapers.

Books. The Card Catalog is your key to finding the information contained in books in any library. Actually, the catalog is an alphabetical file of 3x5 cards arranged by author, subject and title, listing all the books in the library.

When a library receives a new book, one of the librarians or, in the case of large libraries, a cataloger produces the catalog card. This card contains the author's name, his birth date (and if deceased, the year of his death), title of the book, publisher, place and date of publication, and number of pages. It also lists information on whether the volume contains a bibliography, illustrations, maps and plates. Most important of all, the card carries a *classmark* that will enable you to locate it quickly among other books on the same subject.

Here is the Library of Congress Catalog Card for a book that was an important research source for the succeeding chapter of this book.

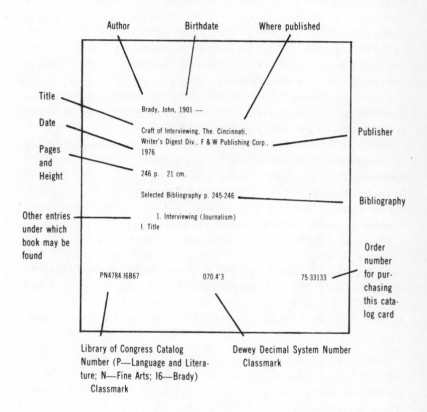

As you can see from the card, this book is also indexed under "Interviewing" and *"Craft of Interviewing, The."* Thus, if you're not familiar with the author, you can still find the book under its general subject matter or title.

Learning to find your way around in libraries is like finding your way around in supermarkets. They are all the same, yet they are all different.

Large libraries may have "closed" shelves and stacks for which you'll be required to fill out a call slip with the author, title and classmark to get the book(s) you want. In smaller libraries you're likely to find an "open" shelves and stacks policy which means you, rather than members of the library's staff, will have to ferret out your own material.

Don't let this worry you. As long as you know the classmark of the book you're looking for, chances are you can find it. At the present time, there are only two classmark systems in general use in American libraries. These are the Dewey Decimal System, used by most public libraries, and the Library of Congress System, which is frequently used by the larger university libraries.

The Dewey Decimal System has ten generic categories under which books are classified. These are:

000-General Works	500-Natural Sciences
100-Philosophy	600-Useful Arts
200-Religion	700-Fine Arts
300-Sociology	800-Literature
400-Philology	900-History and Biography

Instead of numbers, the Library of Congress System utilizes letters to divide books into these 20 broad classifications:

A-General Works	M-Music
B-Philosophy, Religion	N-Fine Arts
C-History	P-Language and Literature
D-Foreign History	Q-Science
E,F-American History	R-Medicine
G-Geography, Anthropology	S-Agriculture
H-Social Sciences	T-Technology
J-Political Sciences	U-Military Science
K-Law	V-Naval Science
L-Education	Z-Library Science, Bibliography

Most libraries have floor plans and signs indicating where you can locate the book you need once you've gotten its classmark, author and title. If you can't find the book, ask for assistance. If the book is in use, most libraries will put a "reserve" on it and notify you by mail when it has been returned.

If a book is unavailable at the library you're in the habit of using, you'll frequently be able to get your hands on it through a process called interlibrary loan. Most major libraries will lend materials to other libraries for periods of up to four weeks, so even though you live in a small town, you can still get most of the research materials you need through the state library or state university libraries. Your local librarian can give you information and the necessary forms to get those books that have eluded you.

In addition to public, state and university libraries, there is another type of library that is often overlooked — the private library. Private libraries are maintained by professional organizations, trade associations, labor unions and charitable foundations. While these collections are ostensibly private, most welcome writers. Many are tremendously cooperative and will often respond to mail requests by photocopying the material you are seeking and forwarding it to you.

The value of these specialized repositories was impressed upon me recently while I was researching this book. I'd spent the better part of five hours in the New York Public Library at the corner of 42nd Street and Fifth Avenue seeking out a bit of obscure information and came up with nothing but a headache from peering at myriad index cards. Now, normally, when you can't uncover a research source in this library, the odds are that it just doesn't exist.

Anyway, I'm a persistent researcher and figured one last shot at one last library might be worth a ten-block walk. I wandered up Lexington Avenue to the Magazine Publisher's Association Library, where, within five minutes after my arrival, I was comfortably seated at a desk with not one source, but three of them!

Over the years, while reading the works of other writers, I've frequently found myself wondering what the *exact* research process was that went into the story. In some stories the process is obvious with many sources named and, in the case of the ones that are not, they can be easily guessed. On the other hand, I often read a piece that perplexes me to the point that I want to write the author to ask him how in hell he carried off his research and how much time he spent at it. I'm certain that everyone interested in writing has had this urge, but I've never read an article in which the writer explained the research methods employed in its writing.

It's time this was done. So, read on, for a reprinted article and notes on its creation.

New England's Mysterious New Animal

Jerome E. Kelley

Have you seen one of those late-night TV chillers where a strange creature shows up, seemingly from out of nowhere? If you live in New England and had looked out your back door while the TV show was playing, you might actually have seen just such a critter rifling your garbage pail.

In the recent past, a new animal has appeared on the local scene, and scientists are still trying to determine the creature's antecedents.

Searched three libraries: the Rutland Public Library; the University of Vermont Library in Burlington; the State Library in Montpelier. (Six hours)

But let's start at the beginning. We only have to go back two decades to do so. In the early 1950s, people in southwestern Vermont began to see coyotes for the first time. This of itself was highly curious. At the time, I made a search of the literature pertaining to fauna of the Green Mountain State and failed to find a single reference to this canid.

Whether or not the coyote had been in Vermont before, it prospered, and it wasn't long before its eerie keening was heard from Massachusetts to the Canadian Border.

Newspaper Clippings.

As the coyote increased its range and numbers, rumors of another, larger animal began to crop up with disconcerting frequency. According to the stories I was hearing, this was a canid twice the size of the coyote but possessing many of the same characteristics. Old-time woodsmen in my area figured that the animal was a cross between domestic dogs and the newly arrived coyotes and took to calling them "coydogs."

The first of these critters I saw was shot during deer season, seventeen years ago, by a good friend in Chittenden, Vermont. From the tip of its bushy tail to its wolf-like nose, it measured close to five feet and weighed just under sixty pounds. In color it was a dark, grizzled, brownish-red. Its underparts—from muzzle to three-quarters of the way up the tail—were almost cream colored.

During the next three or four years I had the opportunity of viewing a dozen or more of these animals and began having some nagging doubts whether the name "coydog" was either apt or accurate. What bothered me particularly was the question—why, if domestic dogs and coyotes were crossbreeding in substantial numbers, hadn't this happened before? To be sure, there were some accounts of these two animals mating, but it was a rarity and not the rule.

Searched literature in Rutland Library for accounts of dogs hybridizing with coyotes. (Two hours)

Then there was the problem of genes. Ever since Gregor Mendel's experiments with peas in the late 1800s laid the foundations for genetic science, it has been known that when you cross two distantly related species, the second generation will exhibit maximum variations of external characteristics.

Used *Encyclopedia Britannica* as reference. (One-fourth hour)

Here was the problem. The animals I'd been seeing didn't have any variations. Except for size and age they were as alike as peas in a pod. I mentioned this to a couple of naturalists and three or four biologists, and what I got for my troubles were the same kind of sympathetic looks that people who think they are Napoleon get from white-coated attendants.

Short interview at University of Vermont and with biologists of Fish and Game Department in Montpelier. (Three hours)

By this time, the so-called coydog was rapidly moving throughout the length and breadth of New England, migrating south into Massachusetts and northern Connecticut and across New Hampshire and into Maine. In 1960 a husband-and-wife team of fish-and-game biologists in New Hampshire, Walter and Helenette Silver, began a straightforward approach in an effort to determine how this animal evolved. They mated a brother and sister that had been dug from a den in Croydon, New Hampshire in April 1960 and found that the resulting pups were perfectly uniform. While

Telephone interviews with Helenette Silver and New Hampshire Fish and Game Department official. (One-half hour)

this experiment didn't entirely explode the coydog hypothesis, it put a good many irreparable dents and cracks in it.

A different approach was employed at Harvard University to trace this animal's family tree. There a group of taxonomists under the direction of Barbara Lawrence and Dr. William Bossert fed a large number of New England canid skull measurements—along with those of dogs, coydogs, coyotes, and wolves—into their computers. The readouts showed that the skull proportions of the New England canid fell somewhere between those of the coyote and the timber wolf.

Correspondence (One hour)

These measurements, coupled with their own studies of behavior among the New England canids, prompted the Silvers to suggest that the animal is a form of coyote and should, therefore, be called eastern coyote (Canis latrans var.). The Silvers suggest that the animal evolved from coyotes with the addition of dog and/or wolf genes.

Doctor Sydney Anderson, curator of the Department of North American Mammals at the American Museum of Natural History, is of the opinion that the New England canids are the descendents of one or more species of canids, chiefly coyotes, but he does not rule out the possibility of some dog mixture.

Telephone interview. (15 minutes)

Meanwhile Dr. Raymond P. Coppinger of Hampshire College in Amherst, Massachusetts has been directing a continuing series of studies focused on dispelling the myth and mystery surrounding this animal. Dr. Coppinger and his assistants have amassed an imposing array of data on behavior, habitat, range, predator-prey relationships, and taxonomy. While some of their research has raised as many questions as it has answered, they are convinced that the New England canid is not a coydog and, as a consequence, they've named it the "new wolf."

Telephone interview and lengthy correspondence. (Two hours)

I can't quibble with the name except on one score. Unhappily, the word "wolf" seems to conjure up unsavory and largely unfounded images in people's minds, but in fact the new wolf, and the timber wolf for that matter, is far from a rapacious killer. If I had to pick three words to describe this handsome animal I'd choose "beneficial," "furtive," and "adaptable."

But let's take a close look at him in order to understand the basis for my choice. When the new wolf or eastern coyote—whatever one calls it—appeared on the scene, farmers were fearful of what would happen to their pastured livestock. As far as I can determine, there are no authenticated incidents where this animal has attacked either cows or horses. There are, however, accounts of new wolves that have been seen foraging for mice in a field occupied by grazing cattle. Neither canids nor cows paid the slightest attention to the other.

Correspondence with Fish and Game Departments in *all* New England states. (Two hours)

There's no denying that, in rare instances, the new wolf has killed sheep; but in a majority of the cases reported, further careful investigations by game wardens point to some nearby domestic dog as the perpetrator.

Most game-management officials in the Northeast agree that the new wolf fills an important predator void that was left by the disappearance of timber wolves. Like its predecessor, the new wolf is an omnivorous predator and, while a good share of its diet is composed of mice and other small rodents, this canid does not rely solely on them for his food. As a matter of fact, when it comes to food, the new wolf could be likened to a four-legged suction pump. Only one other creature rivals him when it comes to a wide range of stomach contents, and that's the shark.

In addition to the flesh, fur, and hide of rodents and other mammals, examination of the stomachs of new wolves has revealed such diverse items as nuts, berries, apples, insects, frogs, snakes, twigs, pebbles, grass, porcupine quills, fish bones, beer-can tops, orange peel, aluminum foil and the netting from an onion bag.

Correspondence with one of Dr. Coppinger's graduate students. (One hour)

The new wolf, like many of us, believes in making a living with a minimum expenditure of energy. Because of this, three of its favored hunting grounds are garbage pails, town dumps, and farmers' manure piles. When not scrounging around these repositories, the canid frequently patrols nearby highways, and the prey in this case is the remains of raccoons, skunks, squirrels, and birds that have been killed by passing vehicles. When hunger drives the new wolf to these middens of civilization for provender, the mission is undertaken under cover of darkness.

Does the new wolf prey on deer? The answer is yes, but with a number of qualifications. Very careful observations by game-management experts indicate that this predator does not go after white-tailed deer to the extent and frequency they had originally anticipated.

When the new wolf turns to deer for sustenance, the victim has usually died of starvation in a winter yard, or been badly wounded by hunters, or is suffering from some infirmity such as disease, old age, or injury that would have soon brought about its demise. The net result of the new wolf's presence in deer country is probably a healthier herd.

For furtiveness, I would have to rank the new wolf right alongside that phantom of the forests—the fisher. I've been observing this canid for seventeen years, have made eighty-eight recorded sightings, and have yet to secure a reproducible photograph of a wild specimen. As of this writing, I haven't heard of anyone else turning this trick with a mature animal. (Photographer Angelo Lomeo thinks that he has managed to capture the beast on film. See above. Ed.)

As far as I can determine, the new wolf is more gregarious than the coyote but much less pack-minded than the timber wolf. In Northern Canada and Alaska I've seen wolf packs comprised of more than twenty animals. The largest number of new wolves I've ever seen running together is seven and, from what I've heard and read, this is an unusually large number. Even in the winter months when one would expect the

Interviews with three game wardens. (Two hours)

The picture was that of a malamute husky!

Article in *Vermont Sportsman*.

packs to become more cohesive, the new wolf frequently hunts alone or with one partner, and I suspect that the reason for this lonely habit has to do with its basic diet—it doesn't take a pack to bring down a field mouse.

A family of new wolves can be pretty wide-ranging. One group I've observed inhabits an area of approximately eighty square miles. Included within this range are some of the most inaccessible mountain areas in Vermont as well as one of the East's largest ski resorts. As large as this area is, the new wolf can generally be found at any given time of the year if one knows where to look.

Verified this by interviewing two other individuals who have been observing this family. (One hour)

In late spring they hang around beaver ponds and other small bodies of water, feasting on small spring frogs. As the berries ripen they head for the brambles on a dual-purpose mission. They like the berries, but they like the birds and small animals that feed on them even better. In August they haunt cornfields in hopes of garnering a meal of corn-fed raccoon. When the nuts begin to ripen, it's off to the hardwood-covered hills. While the new wolf will eat acorns and beechnuts, he's much more interested in the nut-gathering small mammals that abound in such areas.

Personal observation.

With the first frosts, the canid heads for the apple orchards, attracted by the fallen fruit and the small animals that congregate at these windfalls. With the frigid blasts and first snows of winter, the new wolf seeks the alder swamps where mice and unwary cottontail and snowshoe rabbits are the objects of its attention. Late winter finds him in sheltered softwoods close to the deer yards, waiting for the inevitable victims of starvation.

In late February in Vermont, the new wolf starts behaving peculiarly, frolicking one minute and fighting the next. For days he'll be moodily silent. Then suddenly he'll bay, bawl, and howl at the moon for hours, and race from one end of his range to the other without a seeming objective. But there is one: the female of his still indeterminate species. It's breeding season, and like all animals, including *Homo sapiens,* the canid gets a little crazy when sex is in the offing. The gestation period period of the new wolf is short (about nine weeks) and its product small (about three or four pups).

As can be seen, the new wolf is adaptable with a capital A. Some biologists believe that, aside from the skunk, this is the most adaptable animal on this continent. They further believe that it is just this adaptability that has enabled the canid to move so far and so fast in such a short period of time. When first identified, it occupied only a small portion of southwestern Vermont and northern New York. Today, less than twenty years later, the new wolf is at home in every New England state with the possible exception of Rhode Island, and his wanderings have recently taken him into Quebec, New Brunswick, and Pennsylvania.

Interviews and correspondence. (Three hours)

The other day I sat in my kitchen, drinking coffee, musing over the new wolf. I finally decided that he isn't much different from many of us New Englanders. He's not sure who his forebears were. His genealogy is fouled up. He makes his living as best he can, even under some pretty adverse circumstances. He's got lots of nosy neighbors like me. Yet, in spite of this, he survives, and even prospers.

What makes the foregoing story unusual is that I got the idea for it approximately 20 years before I sat down to write it. The research that went into it was picked up piece by small piece during this period. Because my hobbies are hunting, fishing and backpacking, my observations of this animal were generally made while I was engaged in one of these after-writing-hours activities. Similarly, a good deal of the legwork—such as interviews—was undertaken while I was doing research on more immediate stories.

Was the long wait worth it? I've sold two other articles on this animal, so I'm way ahead financially. The real payoff, however, came not long ago when a young lady from Time-Life called me. In a breathless voice she informed me that the Luce empire was putting together an encyclopedia on wildlife. She then proceeded to bombard me with questions on the new wolf.

Finally, I was able to wedge a few words into the one-sided conversation.

"How come you're asking me these questions when there are some real authorities?"

"Oh, don't be modest, Mr. Kelley," she responded brightly. "We've already talked to them and they've all told me you're the real expert!"

See what a little research and patience can do for a writer?

6. Out of the Mouths of Babes and Others

It was one of those sultry summer days in Washington when there wasn't enough news breaking to keep a cub reporter busy. Sam Butz, the prolific freelancer, and I were cosied against the bar of the National Press Club doing our bit for Scotland's balance of payments.

Suddenly, our sodden solitude was broken when a youthful member of the Associated Press Washington Bureau came puffing up to us.

"Chrrrrrist, did you guys hear what Jim Fusca pulled off today?"

"What'd he do now, pick J. Edgar Hoover's office lock?" Sam asked.

"Naw, better than that. We were at the White House for that special NASA briefing, when who pops in but LBJ himself. Anyway, during the briefing, the President goes to the john for a leak and Fusca follows him. One of the Secret Service guys told me that while LBJ was pissing, old Fusca was standing at the next urinal firing questions at him like they were going out of style."

"Did the President unzipper his lip as well as his pants?" I asked.

"You better believe he did. The Secret Service guy claims he answered every damn question. Can you believe it? Whadda headline. I can see it now: 'President Pops While Peeing.' "

We were still digesting this unusual bit of intelligence when Fusca, himself, heaved into view and docked about four feet down the bar.

"Hey, Jim, heard you've been interviewing LBJ in the White House john. How'd it go?" I queried.

Jim removed the ever present briar from his mouth and reflected a moment. We waited expectantly for some choice tidbit. Finally, a small smile flickered across his forlorn spaniel countenance. "Gentlemen," he said, "I can honestly report that our beloved President handled himself very well."

There's a lesson here for would-be interviewers. If you are going to be good at the craft, you've got to use initiative, be persistent and, above all, don't share your information with fellow writers before it gets into print.

A. J. Liebling, who was a reporter's reporter and lucidly chronicled the profession's faults and failures, held the belief that virtually everyone is willing to be interviewed. He once said, "There is almost no circumstance under which an average American doesn't like to be interviewed."

This is one statement of Liebling's that most reporters and writers would argue. It's pretty obvious Liebling never tried to arrange a *tete-a-tete* with the likes of Howard Hughes, Greta Garbo, Daniel K. Ludwig, Jackie Onassis, J. D. Salinger, or Fred Astaire. Of course, it can be reasonably argued whether any of these personalities are or ever were "average Americans."

Getting the Interview

While it's true that 95% of the people in these United States will stand still for an interview, the other five percent are those who cause problems for writers. Unfortunately, the majority of this minority is composed of real newsmakers who've become as wary of writers as a mother musk ox is of an Arctic wolf pack. Even when one is brought to bay, getting any meaningful information can be like trying to play a slot machine with an oyster.

One thing is certain; the successful writer must acquire the subtle skill of interviewing. It's as important as generating story ideas or research and fortunately, interviewing is like many other skills; you get better at it with practice. Chances are you may never feel entirely comfortable poking, prying and sometimes, almost pummeling answers from people, but nonetheless, with patience and practice you can evolve an interview style that will work best for you.

The first chore the interview-bound writer faces is to wrangle an appointment. This is not always an easy trick and may require stealth, patience, persistence and *chutzpa.*

The best line of attack is to make an interview appointment by phoning a week or two in advance. If your phone call results in a *nyet,* follow up with a letter. Explain why the interview is important and, in a general way, what subjects you hope to cover. Don't, at this point, include any direct questions in your communication, for they may scare your quarry off for good. A little flattery, if it's not too obvious, can often grease the way to a personal confrontation. If the potential subject of your interview, however, happens to be an actor, actress, model, or member of the so-called "beautiful people" set, lay the flattery on with a manure fork instead of a trowel.

Let's assume your letter pulls no response or, worse, a negative one. What to do? Simple. Make like a credit collection agency and write another letter—a stronger one. In this letter, you include a paragraph that is almost guaranteed a reply.

For example:

Some weeks ago I phoned you in an attempt to arrange an interview. At that time you declined because of your busy schedule. More recently, I wrote to you explaining why an interview with you was important and delineated some of the areas I hoped we could cover. Thus far, I have not received a reply.

Meanwhile, I have proceeded to gather material for my article. Unfortunately, a good deal of this research tends to place you in an extremely unfavorable light. Obviously, an interview with you could very well give some *important balance* to the piece that may, otherwise, be lacking.

In those rare instances when a letter like this fails, there are still other avenues for the persistent writer. The unauthorized biography of Howard Hughes by Albert P. Gerber is an example. Gerber tried to contact Hughes, but failed. Jean Peters, his former wife, and close business associates were equally inaccessible. Finally, out of desperation, he turned to people who had briefer contacts with the reclusive billionaire. There were literally hundreds of actors, actresses, directors, producers, teachers, barbers, and distant relatives. From interviews with these people, Gerber pieced together a book that gave remarkable insight into the mores, morals and motivations of this hermetic hermit.

Arthur Marx, Groucho's son, recently had an experience similar to Gerber's. He'd started work on an unauthorized biography of Carrol O'Connor, who got wind of the project and placed ads in newspapers warning his friends not to talk to Marx. Even if O'Connor's friends heed his warning, Marx still has an option; he can still interview O'Connor's enemies, of which there are a goodly number. One thing Marx has already proved about O'Connor is that there is more

Archie Bunker in the man than most people suspected.

Magazine editors have long been cognizant of the fact that some people will acquiesce more readily to an interview if the writer with the *right* credentials approaches them. This is the reason that many nonwriters suddenly become writers—high paid writers. Lucy Johnson Nugent, Julie Nixon Eisenhower, and Margaret Trudeau are notable, if not overly-talented, examples.

Your Place or Mine?

Once you've brought your quarry to bay, the next step is to arrange a time and place. While time isn't crucially important, you'd be well advised to opt for an afternoon appointment if your subject is a heavy drinker. Most writers quickly learn that a hangover-ravaged interviewee isn't as productive as one that is bright-eyed and bushy-tailed. On the other hand, if your subject has a penchant for potables, a late afternoon meeting may mean you'll find him already well into his cups. Rex Reed had this experience. He once interviewed Ava Gardner when she was drunk as a skunk. Ava screamed like a banshee when she read the interview. She didn't yell foul and claim she'd been misquoted, she just stopped granting interviews—all interviews.

After you've settled on the time, you must choose the place for the interview. Beware: there is only one place worse than a restaurant for conducting interviews—a bordello. Having never conducted an interview in a bordello, although I know two writers who have, I'll stick to the facts and list the reasons why restaurants are to be shunned. First off, there's the simple question of economics. As the interviewer, it is your responsibility to pick up the tab. Over the years, I've caught my share and some of them were lulus. Invariably, interviewees will select the most expensive place in town, then show up with wives, kids, girlfriends, groupies, or whomever they are trying to impress on that particular day. With drinks, the highest-priced entree on the menu, wine, dessert, after-dinner brandy, and a post-prandial Corona or two, the bill can resemble a junior version of the national debt. It's a bit unnerving to cough up $200 for an interview that isn't worth twenty cents.

Another reason restaurants aren't ideal locations for interviews is the background noise. I once interviewed the president of a large advertising agency in Chandler's in New York City, which is, without a doubt, the noisiest restaurant on the North American Continent. The answers to my first three questions were: "Huh?" "What?" and "Come again?" Looking up, I noted for the first time that my subject had a hearing aid screwed into his left ear. He pointed to it and scribbled on a napkin, "I've got this goddamn thing turned up to full blast and I still can't hear you!" We ate in silence and resumed the interview back in the relative quiet of his office.

Finally, if the subject you happen to interview in a restaurant is a celebrity, even a bush-league one, you're going to have to fend off the public. Trying to bring any order to an interview when the interviewee is autographing menus is a difficult task to say the least.

By far the best spot to tackle most interviews is right in the living room of the interviewee's house, since the subject almost always feels more at ease, more talkative, and more "protected" when in a familiar home environment. There's another plus in interviewing a subject in his own digs. Careful observation can usually give you important clues to your subject's likes, dislikes and lifestyle. This free intelligence often adds much more substance and background to your story.

Regardless of where an interview is held, its success or failure depends, to a large degree, on how carefully the writer researches his subject. Many writers won't go near a subject until they're certain they know 90% of the answers to questions they are going to ask. To accomplish this, they frequently spend more time preparing for an interview than they spend on the interview itself..

Playboy's monthly interviews are classics of careful, painstaking preparation. Eric Norden, who did the interview with ex-Nazi minister Albert Speer, spent nearly two months reading everything Speer had written, as well as everything he could lay his hands on that had been written about Speer.

Robert Scheer no doubt spent even more time than that preparing for his now famous interviews with Jerry Brown and Jimmy Carter. Not only did he sift through all available literature on these two politicians, but he spent an enormous amount of time eliciting input from families, associates, friends and enemies. Scheer approaches his interviewee armed to the teeth with information. But he doesn't necessarily let the interviewee know the extent of his knowledge right off the bat. Says Scheer in an interview in *More:* (March 1977)

> There's no doubt that it's better to be less threatening. But you
> need the killer instinct, too. You ask the dumb question, but at
> some point you have to spring back with the contradictions.
> Otherwise, you'll just end up with little lectures.

In recent years, TV journalists have been employing an approach to research that may have application for writers: the preinterview interview. For his CBS interview with H. R. Haldeman, Mike Wallace reportedly spent 55 hours holding "preliminary discussions" for an interview that turned out to be about as exciting as watching grass grow.

Probably the only time this technique would be effective is when the interviewee is being paid to stand still for an interview. Unfortunately, more and more celebrities are holding out for money before they'll start chirping for publication or TV cameras. Gary Gilmore nailed *Playboy* for a chunk of cash that ran into the high five-figure range and ex-President Nixon is another "Pop off for pay" champion. According to most reports, David Frost had to pony up $500,000 for the privilege of taping a series of interviews with the former president. While writers and editors find "checkbook journalism" distasteful, most are certain the situation will get far worse before it gets better.

Interview Etiquette

How you dress and act can have an important bearing on how the interview goes. Dress neatly and don't try to compete with your subject. Greet him with a firm handshake. Whether you feel it or not, always try to project an air of confidence and competence.

Being punctual for your interview appointment is extremely important. If the time is set for nine, be there at 8:55, not 9:05. I've heard of interviews being cancelled when the writer was a minute or two late. Don't let this happen to you.

Once you and your subject have gotten settled, it's time to discuss the ground rules of the interview—unless the interviewee has already spelled them out. If the subject doesn't bring up the matter, leave well enough alone. Unfortunately, the real newsmakers in this world have become more and more sophisticated when it comes to dealing with writers and frequently impose stringent conditions before they open their mouths. Some interviewees are petrified of tape recorders and won't allow you to unsheathe one in their presence. Others may inform the interviewer that his remarks are going to be "off the record," meaning he's going to sing like the proverbial canary and the interviewer can make use of his remarks, but they cannot be attributed to him. Don't let this get you down. John Kenneth Galbraith once said, "I am persuaded that, with rare exceptions, what must be said off the record had best not be said at all."

Off the record comments often provide the writer with some of the juiciest morsels he can lay his typewriter on. He must weave them into his story and attribute them to a "highly placed official," "a reliable spokesman," "an unimpeachable source," "an unofficial spokesman," "a well-informed observer," "a long-time associate," or "an acknowledged expert." Some writers have been known to take a single, off-the-record interview and attribute it to more than one of the above-named phantoms in the resulting story. Jim Fusca used to call this technique "literary body building."

While most journalists honor off-the-record agreements, there is a small minority that doesn't, providing the material is important enough. Robert Scheer is a case in point. Scheer's feeling is that no matter the circumstances, the writer's obligation is to present the facts. Says Scheer:

I think it's . . . important not to break your word to your readers. There's an implicit understanding when a writer writes for a reader that you're telling the reader what you know. And I'm saying that my bond to myself is that I'm not going to withhold information from my readers.

And if the source of the off-the-record remark is an essential part of the information, then the source's name should be revealed, regardless of the agreement under which the information was obtained, Scheer believes.

Remember: never shy away from an off-the-record interview. "Deep Throat" chirped off the record and made Rob Woodward and Carl Bernstein a ton of money.

The interviewee may insist on yet another ground rule—the opportunity to see final copy before it appears in print. If you want the interview badly enough, you'll probably have to swallow your professional pride and agree. *Playboy* frequently offers this condition to reluctant interviewees. While I'm certain some choice morsels have been excised because of this ground rule, it hasn't affected the overall quality of *Playboy*'s interview efforts.

Questioning Your Quarry

The real pros of interviewing seldom read their questions from a prepared list—they memorize them. Others, whose memories are faulty, use small, inconspicuous crib notes, thus lending an air of informality to an interview which puts the subject at ease, and, hopefully, off guard.

No two writers use exactly the same technique. Matter-of-fact, a few writers use what could be described as a "nontechnique." In his book, *Here at the New Yorker*, Brendan Gill describes how his good friend A. J. Liebling would attack an interview situation:

Liebling had a singular, highly successful method of interviewing people. He would sit facing the person from whom he intended to elicit information; and then sit there and sit there, silently. Soon the person being interviewed would begin to break down. Most reporters plunge into the interview asking too many questions, among which the interviewee is forced to pick and choose, concentrating upon questions that are the easiest to deal with and skirting without seeming to do so those that might prove embarrassing to him. Liebling's method left the interviewee unnerved and at a loss as to what he was expected to defend himself against; by the time Liebling had put the first question to him, he was ready to babble almost any indiscretion.

Another low-key interview approach is the one used by long-time Washington-based writer, Sam Butz. For lack of a more precise term, let's call it the "good old boy" technique. Sam has a wondrous southern drawl, a steel trap mind and he blushes easily. During an interview, he speaks in a soft, unhurried voice. When he arrives at a tough question, he pauses. His face turns crimson and he prefaces his question with, "Ahhh sure kind of hate to ask you this, but I reckon I've got to. It's kind of important. So, here goes."

At this point, Sam lowers his voice and almost whispers the question. The interviewee, sensing Sam's acute discomfort, rushes to his aid with the answer and in the process usually says more than he intended to. This technique has disarmed politicians, scientists, generals, sports figures, and newsmakers of just about every other persuasion.

George Cushman, another long-time writing acquaintance, uses what might be accurately termed the "schoolboy enthusiasm" technique. George approaches each interview as though it was his first. His eyes flash with excitement, his voice frequently cracks and his delivery is rapid-fire Jerry Lewis. Interviewees get infected by his bubble gum snapping, "Oh boy!" technique and before they know it, they, too, are chirping.

From time-to-time, a writer appears on the scene who possesses some undefinable, almost occult capacity for getting people to say things they didn't want to say, and more importantly, probably shouldn't have said. One of these is the Italian writer, Oriana Fallaci. Watching Fallaci from across a restaurant as she sparrow picks her food, it is a bit difficult to understand how this almost fragile creature has become the big shot's *bete noire.*

She dresses—usually in black— with studied casualness. Her straight hair is long, infrequently combed and wreathes a finely-wrought, oval face with high cheekbones and sensuous full lips that are cast in a perpetual, petulant pout. As she talks, her hands are sadly expressive. From a distance, she exudes, indeed almost projects, an air of weary vulnerability that is more than a little reminiscent of Edith Piaf.

Many Fallaci watchers, and there's a horde of them, believe that it is this waif-like presence she brings to her interviews that allows her to return home with the bloody scalps of such notables as Henry Kissinger, Nguyen Van Thieu, Hugh Hefner, Alfred Hitchcock, Frederico Fellini, The Shah of Iran and countless others hanging from her Gucci belt.

While this may, in part, be true, Fallaci does long hours of homework to bring to her interviews questions that are relevant, tough, hard-nosed and explosive. Her interview with the then Secretary of State, Henry Kissinger, is something of a classic. Here was a Ph.D from Harvard, a former professor and a man highly gifted in the manipulative, evasive and crafty skills of diplomacy pitted against an almost forlorn girl whose English could best be described as engagingly broken.

While such a match would seem to be no contest, it didn't turn out that way. Fallaci's pivotal question in this interview was almost Machiavellian: "Dr. Kissinger . . . how do you explain the fact that you have become almost more famous and popular than a President? Have you any theories?"

The Secretary of State hedged, but only momentarily. When he finally responded, it was with this nugget of pure interviewer's gold:

. . . I've always acted alone. Americans admire that enormously. Americans admire the cowboy leading the caravan alone astride his horse, the cowboy entering a village alone on his horse. Without even a pistol, maybe, because he doesn't go in for shooting. He acts, that's all; aiming at the right spot at the right time. A wild West tale if you like.

For a while the press called the Secretary of State "High Noon Henry." The American taxpayer was a bit disconcerted to learn that its foreign policy was being formulated and implemented by a "cowboy," while the reaction within the White House to the Secretary's remarks was distinctly frigid. On reading the interview the Secretary was heard to remark, "I couldn't have said those things. It's impossible; impossible!"

If this was his only defense, it was a mighty specious one. The interview had been recorded!

The first questions of an interview should be much like the "warm-up" period of a TV show. They're intended to get the subject into the frame of mind for what's to come. No experienced interviewer ever pops the money questions up front.

Shortly after Calvin Coolidge left the White House, an enterprising reporter for one of Washington's largest newspapers finally succeeded in arranging an interview with the recently departed president. Instead of trying to warm up the taciturn Yankee, who richly deserved his nickname "Silent Cal," the young lady conducting the interview fired her big guns first. Here's the so-called interview in its stark entirety:

Reporter: Mr. President, how do you feel since you left the presidency?

C. C.: Relaxed.

Reporter: Mr. President, now that you're leaving Washington
            what do you plan to do?
C. C.:   Loaf.
Reporter: (in desperation): Mr. President, what were your final
            words when you left the White House?
C. C.:   I told Grace (Mrs. Coolidge) not to forget my rub-
            bers.

As the warm-up proceeds, the interviewer gains insight into how quickly he can start laying on the heavy questions. For some subjects this can take an hour or more, while others will start spouting like Moby Dick almost at the outset.

Most experienced writers like Edward Linn, Alex Haley, Hal Higdon and Max Gunther use a general question as their warm-up. This has the advantage of allowing the subject to take off in any direction. It also gives the interviewer an indication of where his subject's interests lie. As the interviewee travels down the broad verbal path of the general question, the interviewer brings fuzzy generalities into close focus by asking such questions as: "Could you elaborate on that?"; "Would you give me some details?"; "Can you give me an example?". Some writers swear that the carefully-thought-out, well-phrased general question can lead right to the end of a successfully concluded interview. This may be true, but the interviewer is going to have to employ many interrogatories along the way.

Some expert interviewers recommend that you preface your general warm-up question with the word *when,* since this puts the subject into the time period you prefer. Succeeding interrogatories are then prefaced by the interviewer's "who," "what," "where" and "why." If this approach is employed, the resulting article may be relatively easy to write.

Anecdotes—good anecdotes—add color and reader interest to the story while at the same time they provide insights into the subject's personality. I doubt if any interviewer has ever concocted a sure-fire way of dredging up these highly-prized gems, but there is one technique Hal Higdon uses that is well worth trying. "Recite an anecdote you have already collected on the subject at hand," suggests Higdon. "Often the person you're interviewing will respond to this challenge by trying to top you with a better example."

The Camera Sees All

There is one type of interviewing technique that should be avoided by writers. This is the TV or "sandbag" approach that is employed, often profitably, by TV journalists such as Howard Cosell, Mike Wallace, Morely Safer, Dan Rather and Barbara Walters.

The choreography of the "sandbag" technique is like that of a barn cat stalking a mouse in a haymow. The interviewer begins gently, almost quietly asking innocuous questions that are easily answered. The tense interviewee begins to feel comfortable and gains confidence that he will be able to field any questions strewn in his path. The interviewer adds to this euphoric calm by continuing to cast "soft" questions. Suddenly the loaded question descends on the interviewee with all the finality of an unsheathed claw.

With three cameras pointed down the interviewee's throat, the guy or gal in the hot seat has only two options—answer the question or clam up. Either way he'll probably end up sounding or looking like a jerk.

With cameras recording their every twitch and audio equipment recording every weasel-word, there is absolutely no place for the interviewee to hide.

When a writer tries to use this technique, though, he's asking for disastrous results. At best, the interviewee will simply button his lip and terminate the interview. At worst, the interviewer can become the subject of an aggravated assault. The problem of course, is that the action of the interviewee is not constricted by a battery of cameras and a national TV audience.

Getting Tough

When an interview starts to bog down, with answers becoming more evasive and nebulous, it's time for the interviewer to get tough. Actually, he has no other choice except to pack his satchel and leave. Getting tough, however, doesn't mean being antagonistic; nor does it mean shoving bamboo splinters under the subject's fingernails.

Asking tough qestions without any varnish on them may work for TV interviewing, but, as we've mentioned, it seldom works for the writer/interviewer. If a writer decides to shove a verbal fist into his subject's face, he had better cover it with a little velvet. Here's how:

The rumor question: "There's a rumor pretty prevalent in New York these days, and I'm sure you've heard it, that your marriage is falling apart. Is it true?" If the subject insists she's happily married, the astute interviewer can still pursue this line and possibly make some hay out of it by asking, "Who in the world would want to damage your reputation by starting such a rumor and why?"

The I want to help you appeal: "Recently, I read that you're considered a miser by some, if not all, of your close business associates. Here's your opportunity to answer them in print."

I'm only passing a question along question: "A lot of people are questioning your sanity because you married a girl 42 years younger than you. Would you like to answer these critics?"

The flattery will get you somewhere question: "Over the years you've gained an enviable reputation for candor, so would you give us the *real* reasons why you murdered your wife, your mother-in-law, and the family dog?"

The what if question: "What if your wife's father disinherits her as he's implied? How are you going to maintain your present lavish style of living?" The "what if" question will also work if it's prefaced with a "let's assume," "hypothetically," "supposing" or "looking down the road."

The double-barreled question: "Over the years, you've uttered innumerable cynical remarks with regard to love and marriage. Is this correct?" Subject nods and interviewer fires the second barrel. "Then if these remarks are true, I can only assume that your upcoming marriage is for money. Is *this* correct?"

The question of degree question: "Many writers are heavy users of alcohol. Would you categorize yourself as a heavy drinker, a medium-heavy drinker, a moderate drinker, a social drinker or a teetotaler?"

The euphemistic question: "You've a reputation for being one of the world's great lovers. Do you ascribe your good fortune with the fair sex to your wealth, your talent, your good looks, your personality or do you have some other endowment you've kept hidden from the public?"

If none of these work, then you'll have to fall back on the type of question that lawyers have been using since Blackstone was a boy—the leading question. In its classic form it goes like this, "Do you feel the disclosure of your financial losses related to poor judgment has a place in your political campaign?" A word of warning. Before you drop one of these bombs on an unsuspecting subject, make sure you have your coat on and are close to the door.

7. Getting it Together

A good magazine article, whether you toiled for weeks researching it or popped it off the top of your head in a matter of hours, must be built on a firm foundation. It should read as if all the facts, anecdotes, examples, and quotes fit together smoothly, flowing from one conclusion to another until the piece reaches its logical end.

Let's take a look at what we've already determined is the easiest type of article to write—the nonresearch variety. Here, the writer gets an idea for a story and all the information he needs to crank it out is already in his cranium.

One sunny morning in the spring of 1974 I was doddling over a second cup of coffee trying to stoke up enough ambition to get my butt behind the typewriter and attack an assignment I wasn't terribly enthused about. I was still working up my ambition when I heard the postman pull up to the rural mailbox in front of my house in Vermont. Retrieving its sparse contents—a manuscript check and a copy of *Reader's Digest*—I returned to my coffee and started to thumb through the *Digest*.

I started from the front of the book, and noted with amazement that the rates for the paragraph-long items used in Humor in Uniform, Campus Comedy, All in a Day's Work, and Life in These United States had been raised from $100 to $200.

I'd never submitted a piece to the *Digest* before, but that morning I hustled off to my typewriter, cranked in a sheet of paper and in less than two minutes had rapped out this paragraph:

> In the early days of World War II, at the age of 17, I ran away from home in Montpelier, Vermont, and enlisted in the Black Watch of Canada. On my first leave, I returned home wearing the kilt of my famous regiment. One evening we had company, and I was sitting in the living room talking to our guests. My mother, who had been preparing supper, came in from the kitchen. Taking one look at me, she said, "Son, if you're going to be a soldier, you've got to learn to sit like a lady!"

As I addressed the envelope to the Humor in Uniform Editor, I felt modest satisfaction. That sixth sense that most old freelancers develop told me that the piece would see print.

As I thumbed on through the magazine I came to a First Person Award Story, for which the *Digest* pays $3,000. I read it carefully and noticed something that had escaped my attention during the many years I had read the publication.

The structure of the piece seemed to me, at least, to be startlingly simple—almost too simple! On a scratch pad I outlined it as follows:

A. A problem exists.

B. The problem intensifies.

C. The problem is solved.

An idea for a *First Person Award Story* began to ricochet inside my head. It had obviously been triggered off by the Humor in Uniform item I'd just written which had brought a host of old Canadian Army memories flooding back after a drought of three decades.

In order to verify my discovery about story structure, I got out a stack of *Reader's Digests* from a closet. Reading the ones I had been able to find indicated that I had been almost 100% correct about their story structure. The only minor difference was that in some cases, the problem wasn't fully solved, but was ameliorated to the point that the person or persons involved could live with it. I didn't waste any time setting down on paper an outline for a story that, for the last half-hour, had been caroming in my head.

Outlines—for both research and nonresearch pieces—are like road maps; by following them the writer will not stray off his path onto detours that lead to verbal thickets of obscurity and minutia.

The following is the original outline (in the margins) together with the story, which took less than three hours to write, as it appeared in *Reader's Digest.*

The Pied Piper of "A" Company

by Jerome E. Kelley

Problem.
Turned down by Marine Corps early in World War II for being flat-footed, underweight and under-age. Run away from home and join Canadian Army.

My story begins in a Marine Corps recruiting office in Montpelier, Vt., a few days after Pearl Harbor. The square-jawed recruiting sergeant sat behind his scarred, wooden desk, tapping with his pencil as he looked me up and down. When he finally spoke, the tapping cadence seemed to underline every word: "Kelley, the Marine Corps is turning you down. First, you're only 17 and you don't have your parents' consent. Second, you're 20 pounds underweight. Third, you have the *flattest* feet the doctor has ever seen!" And he started to laugh.

That did it. "Let me tell *you* something!" I exploded. "You'll still be a three-striped pencil pusher on recruiting duty in Montpelier when I'm overseas with a fighting outfit!"

"Oh, ho!" he chuckled. "I'll bet a month's pay on *that.*"

That night I ran away from home. And the following day, lying about my age, I enlisted in the Canadian army in Montreal.

Problem Intensifies.
Go overseas and join regular unit—1st Battalion Black Watch. On first day our company is sent on five-day field exercise. The company commander tells us, before starting the 30-mile march to exercise

The weeks of infantry training in Quebec weren't too tough. And life at the replacement depot in southern England was even softer. Mostly we played cards or wandered around the English countryside. Then came the day of reckoning—posting to our regular units. The driver dropped me off in front of a row of decrepit houses on a desolate stretch of Sussex coast.

"Well, good luck," he said cheerfully. "They claim this is the toughest outfit in the Canadian army." He waved merrily as he drove off.

I heaved my bag onto my shoulder and staggered toward a building labeled "H.Q., A Company, 1st Battalion, Black Watch of Canada." Inside, a craggy-faced sergeant major briefly studied my records, then, leaving me standing stiffly at attention, departed through a door to his right.

"Sir," I heard him say, "we've just received a replacement."

"*A* replacement? Good Lord! We indent for eight replacements and they send us *one*. What is he—Superman?"

"Hardly, sir. He weighs 125 pounds and has barely a whisker. He'll be the smallest lad in the company. Also, sir, he's flat-footed."

I heard a snort. "Post him to Lieutenant Dorrance's platoon and inform the lieutenant that the new replacement will go with the rest of the company on the Kingley Vale exercise this afternoon."

Two hours later, in full marching order that included 60-pound packs, A Company fell in. Whatever lay in store for us wasn't exciting much joy in the ranks. "Here we go again, fifth exercise in six weeks!" . . .

"Wonder how come he missed a week?" . . . "Third time my leave's been canceled." . . . "Kingley Vale?" . . . "I shoulda joined the Navy . . . ."

"Ten-*shun!*" an officer barked.

The barrel-chested company commander, Maj. Philip Griffin, marched up and down in front of the company for a solid three minutes before he spoke. "It's come to my attention that many of you think these exercises are unnecessary. You're wrong! Soon you will meet the German army in combat. The toughest, best trained troops will win and suffer the fewest casualties. Therefore, whether you like it or not, *you* are going to

area, that since the company was activated no member had fallen out of line of march. He was obviously talking to me. Barely make march. During five rainy days of maneuvers develop acute case of homesickness as well as severe case of infection in feet and shoulders. On eve before return march am certain I'll never make it.

be the toughest, best-trained company in the Canadian army. It's as simple as that!"

The major positioned himself directly in front of me. "Just one more thing!" he shouted, his piercing eyes sizing me up. "Since this company was activated in 1939, no member has fallen out of a line of march. That record will not—repeat, will *not* —be blemished!"

With no further ceremony, A Company marched off behind its two bagpipers and single drummer, to the tune of "Scotland the Brave,"

The torturous nine-hour march to Kingley Vale was only the prelude to five days of sheer, uninterrupted misery. It was night attack, advance, withdrawal, night patrol, platoon attacks, company attacks, firing, guard duty, poor food, cold food, no food, infiltration, wire cutting, demolition, river crossings. And rain. Four days of cold, bone-chilling rain. During all of this time no one spoke to me except to issue an order.

On the night before the return march I huddled under my poncho, wet, muddy and shivering. I was discouraged and scared. Tomorrow would be my 18th birthday. I kept thinking of my family back in Montpelier, and of the birthday cakes my mother used to bake. For once I was glad it was raining. The rain camouflaged my tears.

"Mind if I draw up a chunk of mud and sit?" someone asked. It was Keay, one of the company's bagpipers. "How's it going?"

For the next hour I unburdened myself to Piper Keay. I told him about being an American, about the Marine sergeant in Vermont, about my running away and lying about my age, and how tomorrow would be my 18th birthday. Finally I said, "I'm scared!"

"Scared of what?"

"Scared that tomorrow I'm going to be the first member of A Company ever to fall out of a line of march."

I told him of the running sores on my shoulders caused by my web equipment, and how the broken

Problem is Solved. Bagpiper, who doubles as medic befriends me.

blisters on my feet had become infected. He thought a moment. "Those your blankets?" He pointed to a sodden pile beside me. I nodded. He picked them up. "Stay put," he said. "I'll be right back."

He returned carrying a poncho-wrapped bundle and his medical kit. In those days, pipers and drummers doubled as medics. "Take off your boots and socks," he ordered as he rammed a thermometer into my mouth. Reading the thermometer by flashlight, he clucked, shook three tablets out of a bottle and growled, "Swallow 'em!" Next, he disinfected and bandaged my raw feet. "Here, put on these dry socks."

"Where'd you get dry socks?"

"Same place I got dry blankets," he said, nodding to the poncho-wrapped bundle. "The quartermaster sergeant likes a tot of medicinal rum once in a while. Now, let's get those sores on your shoulders fixed."

In the chow line next morning, Piper Keay was behind me, a bright smile creasing his leathery face. "Still scared?" he asked.

"Yup!"

"Well, you're going to make this march, because Piper Keay is going to make certain you do!"

Fifty minutes marching, 10-minute halt; 50 minutes marching, 10-minute halt. The miles fell slowly away as tired, muddy A Company plodded toward home. After the third hour my feet began to bleed. Sergeant McCallum, my platoon sergeant, fell in beside me. "Feet bleeding, Kelley?"

"Yes, sergeant."

"Piper Keay figured they would. At the next halt take off your boots and Keay will fix you up. Meanwhile, I want you to know you're doing a good job."

The kind words from the sergeant were like medicine. At the next halt Keay rebandaged my feet. Then he handed me a small bottle. "Drink this!"

I forced down the contents and started to gag. "What's that?"

Through his good offices, which include listening to my troubles, treating my infection and playing *Yankee Doodle* on his pipes, I complete march.

Much later receive my commission, return home and meet Marine Corps recruiting sergeant who turned me down. Told him he could shorten the war by recruiting bagpipers because they could make soldiers out of flat-footed, underweight, underage kids overnight.

"Your birthday drink. Some rum the Q.M. sergeant didn't get last night. It'll keep you going for another hour."

During the next 50 minutes, when he wasn't playing his pipes, Keay seemed to be all over the line of march. I saw him speak to Lieutenant Dorrance, then to a big private named Berry and, finally, to the sergeant major. The sergeant major moved up alongside Major Griffin. They talked a moment. The major nodded his head and actually smiled.

The next segment of march was one I dreaded. It was my turn to carry the 22-pound Bren gun. During the halt I went forward to get it from Berry. He eyed me up and down. "It's my turn to carry the Bren," I said.

"It's your birthday, ain't it?"

"Yes, but . . ."

"But what? For a birthday present, the section's decided you lose your turn"

I started to protest. "Shut up!" Berry snarled. Then he smiled. "And happy birthday!"

As we drew abreast of the clock tower on High Street in Chichester, there was a loud flourish on the drum and then the skirling of pipes. I heard it, but I didn't believe it. The pipes were playing "Happy Birthday"! Lieutenant Dorrance gave me a pat on the back. "Happy birthday, Kelley! Only five more miles to go."

They say the last mile is the hardest. Well, I'm a believer. By the time we came to within sight of our billets, blood was oozing out of my boots and was running down both arms from my lacerated shoulders. Spots shimmered in front of my eyes, and I was staggering. *Keep going. One more step. Don't fall.* I kept repeating these words over and over to myself. Then I heard the pipes again. They were playing a tune that, I'm certain, bagpipes had never played before, and it carried me those last, painful 500 yards. The melody was ragged but unmistakable. They were playing "Yankee Doodle."

When the command "Dismissed" was given, I slumped to the ground. Suddenly a form loomed over me.

"Kelley!" I recognized the voice as Major Griffin's and tried to get to my feet. "As you were!" A hand reached down and gripped one of mine. "Happy birthday, Kelley. Show the guts you've shown today and one day you'll have your commission."

Two years later, the major's prediction came true. I was sent to officers' training school in Canada and received my commission. One day, while on leave before re-embarkation, I was walking down State Street in Montpelier when I spotted my old friend—the Marine recruiting sergeant—coming toward me. Even from a distance I could see him eyeing me curiously. Watching his face was like watching a kaleidoscope. Recognition, surprise, amazement and disbelief flashed over it. A few paces from me he snapped the smartest salute I'd ever received. I returned it and let him pass before I barked, "Sergeant!"

He wheeled about. "Sir?"

"Sergeant," I said, "my name is Kelley. I was wondering if you happened to have a month's pay on you."

"Kelley? Oh, ah, er, yes sir! There was a bet, wasn't there, sir?"

"Right, sergeant. But let's forget it. I got over being mad at the Marine Corps years ago. Matter of fact, I'd like to give you Marines a suggestion that might hasten the end of the war. You ought to recruit bagpipers. A good bagpiper can make a soldier out of an under-aged, underweight, flat-footed kid overnight."

I left the good sergeant standing in the middle of State Street, looking perplexed.

There you have it; a simple outline, a simple story and a $3,000 manuscript check. I might also mention that I got another $200 for The Humor in Uniform Piece. In case you think this $3,200 for about three hours work came awfully easy, I'd agree. I'd also hasten to add that you won't stumble across many nonresearch pieces that pay this kind of loot during your writing career. Matter-of-fact, you'll stumble across precious few nonresearch pieces, period! Most stories will be of the research variety, which can certainly pose problems when it comes to outlining.

Outlining the Research Article

As your pile of raw material for an article requiring extensive research grows, you're going to notice some omissions. At this point, it's a good idea to put Ma Bell and the United States Postal Service to work for you. You'll save time and lots of money.

Let's assume in one of your interviews the name of a person is mentioned who, obviously, can furnish you with important information. If you feel you only need to ask him four or five questions, call him. Explain what you're up to, why you need the information, and ask your questions. You'll find that some people will give an interview over the phone more quickly than if you try to arrange a personal meeting.

If your list of questions is longer, send a letter. Remember, a little flattery in the first paragraph will frequently insure a response. If you don't receive a reply within a reasonable time, follow up with a phone call. Explain that you're working against a deadline and the information you seek is crucial to your story. I've found this sob story usually works.

Hopefully, you've been keeping all raw materials in a large envelope, file folder or legal folder. If you—like most writers—are working on several pieces at once, you'll find that keeping all your material for a single story in one, easily-accessible place will make your life much easier and prevent you from misplacing or losing important items. If you can afford a file cabinet to store your "works in progress" materials, you'll find it a good investment.

In getting ready for the actual chore of writing, you should first transcribe notes you've taken during interviews, then transfer the parts you are going to use onto those same 5X8 cards you used for your library research. If you use a free-form shorthand like I do, you'd be well-advised to do your transcribing on the day of the interview. After a couple days, I've found transcribing cold notes a real challenge. Similarly, if you've used a tape recorder, you should also transcribe the parts of the interview you are going to use onto those 5X8 cards. A word of warning: Never throw away your research cards, interview notes or tapes until a reasonable time after your piece appears in print. There are good reasons for this. First, an editor may want to question you about your sources, or the authenticity of a quote. Several years ago I wrote an article and the editor passed it along to an "expert" for his comments. The so-called expert raised 30 questions. Because I'd kept all my research and interview notes, I was able to defend myself on every single point that had been raised. I might add that my rebuttal to the questions was longer than the article itself. It goes without saying that it will be a cold day in hell before I send this editor another manuscript.

Finally, there's the possibility that you might get sued for libel or plagiarism and these materials will prove valuable in your defense. While queries from editors are common and lawsuits are rare, it's a good idea to be prepared for either eventuality.

Very often you'll get the idea for a research piece, but all it'll be is an unstructured idea. You won't have much of an inkling about the proper form and direction for the story until you finish your preliminary research. Even after you've gathered considerable material, the story can suddenly move in an entirely different direction than the one you'd anticipated.

During the summer of 1975, I had an assignment to write the Bicentennial Edition of Vermont's Official Tour Guide. Gathering the material for this book necessitated traveling nearly every highway and byway of the Green Mountain State. One day while negotiating a rural rutted road, I noticed an elderly gentleman panning for gold in a nearby brook. Seeing someone sloshing a gold pan in Vermont was, for me at least, like spotting a roving band of Sioux Indians hunting buffalo in the Bronx Zoo. It was a story possibility—perhaps a good one.

I clambered out of my car, snapped a few photos and began firing questions at the old codger with the gold pan.

"Having any luck?"

"Not much."

"Been panning for gold long?"

"For quite a spell."

"Ever make a strike?"

"Nothing to brag over."

"What's the price of gold now?"

"Dunno."

It was obvious I wasn't going to wring much useful information out of this bird, so I got back into my car and went about my business. For the next two or three weeks I kept my eyes on the brooks and rivers and noticed a sizable number of amateur miners. It was apparent that the skyrocketing price of gold was creating a mini-goldrush in the Green Mountains. When I had a spare moment or two I'd undertake a little research directed toward fleshing out a story on the Yankee yellow metal.

In a few days, I had a sparse handful of those 5x8 cards filled out with enough information to get a handle on the story. Here are the sources, the information, and the sequence in which it was acquired:

Card 1 - Talk With My Mother.

This salty septuagenarian is a walking treasure trove of Vermont lore. Got information from her that a great uncle of mine had found nugget the size of a robin's egg.

Card 2 - Interview With Sports Shop Owner.

Gave me information on gold pans and other equipment.

Card 3 - Wall Street Journal.

Story on current and future gold prices.

Card 4 - Rutland Library.

Information on early gold mining activities in the Massachusetts Bay Colony.

Card 5 - University of Vermont Library.

Information on gold mining in the Plymouth and Bridgewater, Vermont areas.

Card 6 - Master's Thesis; University of Vermont.

Type of gold found in Vermont and information on recent assays.

Card 7 - State Geologist's Office.

Information on where gold has been found and is currently being found.

Card 8 - Interview With "Miner".

Gave me information on how to build and operate a sluice box.

Card 9 - Interview With Friend.

Heard about friend who had supposedly made a strike. Until I had started work on the story I wasn't even aware he'd been panning gold for ten to twelve years.

Card 10 - State Library (Montpelier).

Information on earliest authenticated gold finds in Vermont.

As I shuffled these cards around getting ready to develop a short outline, it occurred to me that I had the makings of a good solid how-to piece, rather than the more pedestrian and harder-to-sell news story I'd expected. I outlined the story right off the cards. Here is the outline (in margins) along with the actual story that appeared in *Yankee Magazine's Guide to New England:*

Panning for Gold
The fun is in the search
by Jerome E. Kelley

Growth of gold panning in Vermont and price of gold. Card 3.

Gold! That magical word that starts blood racing and hopes soaring has been reverberating throughout the beautiful Green Mountains of Vermont with increasing intensity these past two years.

There's gold in Vermont - quite possibly lots of it. Currently the market price fluctuates at around $125 per ounce. Some monetary experts are forecasting that in time, it could conceivably reach the astronomical sum of $250 or $300 per ounce.

This past summer literally hundreds of amateur miners dotted the streams and rivers of Vermont, sloshing their gold pans, looking for that big strike. They ranged in age from toddlers to grandparents. As the price of gold climbs, their numbers are bound to increase. Some observers predict that the way the sport (if that's the proper word) has been growing, it could develop into a full-fledged gold rush by this coming summer.

Colonial efforts to find gold. Card 4.

Gold has a history in New England, going back in time to the days of early settlement. Our Pilgrim fathers came to these rocky shores to find freedom of worship and not gold. Be that as it may, these stern-visaged pragmatists weren't exactly oblivious to what the yellow metal could do for them. Consequently, from time to time, they searched for it in an unorganized fashion.

There are several accounts of where early colonists thought they had struck it rich. Sending their finds to England for assaying, they got back bad news: their "gold" turned out to be iron pyrites, better known as fool's gold.

Over the years the theory came to be accepted that gold was a warm-weather metal, common only to tropical and sub-tropical climates. So early New Englanders gave up prospecting and occupied their time by farming, raising large families, bearding the British and fomenting a revolution.

When gold was finally discovered, it didn't have the effect that one would expect. In 1826, a nugget weighing eight-and-a-half ounces was picked up on the banks of the West River in Newfane, Vermont. It hardly caused a stir, much less excitement in the small community. The reason was simple. A family of notorious counterfeiters - the Wheelers - lived in the vicinity and the local citizenry figured they were the ones who had lost the nugget.

This premise still survives in the Newfane area to this day, but there is room for reasonable doubt. Gold is presently being panned in both the West and Rock rivers in Newfane!

In 1833, Professor Edward Hitchcock of Amherst College was engaged in a geological survey for the State of Massachusetts. While conducting this survey he wandered into Somerset, Vermont, near the Bay State's northern border, and discovered small amounts of gold in some of the neighboring streams. His findings were duly reported in obscure journals and monographs, but went totally unnoticed by potential gold-seekers.

During the 1849 gold rush, thousands of young New Englanders left the rocky hills of home and headed for the California diggings. By the middle 1850's some of them came drifting back from the West.

The Plymouth/Bridgewater gold rush. Card 5.

One of them was an unnamed lad from Plymouth, Vermont. Tradition has it that he returned from the gold fields with a fair-sized poke. In 1855, while fishing in Buffalo Brook, he found a small nugget. Using the knowledge he'd gained in California he was soon working his gold pan overtime on the Buffalo Brook shores.

Secrets in a small New England town in that faraway

day were no different than they are now, and it wasn't long before the word was out and the rush was on.

No one has any accurate idea of how much gold was taken out of the Plymouth area in those days, but geologists at the University of Vermont term it as "considerable." What few records do exist will surely whet the appetites of present-day goldseekers. One miner panned something more than $2,800 of gold out of Plymouth's Gold Brook in one day during the summer of 1858.

Later that same year more than $42,000 worth of the yellow metal was sluiced out of a nearby mill pond. As late as 1884, it is reported that approximately $78,000 worth of ore was taken out of a newly-opened mine in Plymouth during a six-month period.

Gold fever in the Green Mountain State reached its crisis stage in 1885. That year a number of mines were dug in the Raymond Hill and Freestop Hill areas, north of Plymouth in Bridgewater. None of them produced any appreciable amounts of gold and the fever almost, but not quite, died out.

Over the years there have always been a few old-timers who did "a mite of panning" to supplement their incomes. Most of these venerable miners are closed-mouthed Yankees, so we have no record of whether any of them has ever struck it rich or, indeed, has ever made a modest strike.

Inferences, however, can be drawn. Some of these old-timers have been sloshing their gold pans around for 40 or 50 years. It's pretty logical to assume that they've been turning up something more than black fly bites, wet feet and aching backs.

Vermont gold. Cards 1 and 6.

Most of the gold found in the Green Mountain State is referred to by geologists as "placer gold." The metal has been leached out of surrounding rock formations by weather and stream erosion. Because of its high specific gravity and ability to withstand weathering and alteration, it concentrates in stream sediment.

For some unexplicable reason, Vermont gold is purer than gold found in most other parts of the United States. Recent assays indicate the gold runs something on the order of 23-1/2 carats. In layman's language, this means it is roughly 96 percent pure!

Good-sized nuggets aren't common but neither are they rare. A great-uncle of ours found one the size of a robin's egg many years ago in Shady Rill Brook, just north of Montpelier. Recently we've seen three others that were nearly as large.

Most current gold-seekers in the Green Mountains use pans. Hardware and sporting goods stores carry several types ranging from children's models made of plastic to the classic western pan. Prices range from $2 to $7.

How to pan for gold. Cards 2 and 8.

A good panning technique requires patience and practice. The best way to learn is to get an old-timer to show you how it's done. Failing this, read the directions that come with most pans — carefully.

To increase your production — if you are planning to become a gold seeker — you can construct a simple sluice box. All you need is a long, narrow box open at both ends and top. Lathing is nailed at six- or eight-inch intervals across the bottom and this, in turn, is covered by a strip of old carpet.

The sluice box is placed on an incline in the stream in such a way that the water flows through it. Stream sediment is then shoveled onto the top end and, by adjusting the water flow, the light materials will be washed downstrean. The heavier materials such as gold, magnetite and garnet will settle on the carpet.

When the carpet is saturated with heavy materials it is rinsed out in a bucket or old wash tub. This is then transferred to a pan for final panning. The gold remaining is tweezed or spooned into a jar or bottle. Don't use a leather poke — it can leak!

For non-do-it-yourselfers, ready-made sluice boxes manufactured of high-impact plastic are available in many sporting goods stores for around $25. More

How much are the miners making? Card 9.

affluent gold-seekers can purchase a gasoline-powered, dredge-sluice box combination that retails for $275.

Now for the big question. Are present day goldseekers striking it rich in Vermont? No one really knows and the gold-seekers surely aren't telling. There are two reasons: income taxes and competition. A close friend of ours may be pretty typical. He's been panning for 10 or 12 years and has been recently showing some signs of newly acquired affluence. He has just purchased an expensive new camper, has got a fancy, custom-built deer rifle on order and his wife has changed her beauty shop schedule from once a month to twice a week.

Insofar as he doesn't play the stockmarket and he hasn't been the beneficiary for any wills lately, it's obvious he's made a strike and a darned good one at that.

Instead of pussy-footing around we fired the question straight at him. "Ed, we're doing an article on gold panning. It's obvious you've made a good strike. Now level with us. How much did you hit and where'd you hit it?"

He gave me that old hand-in-the-cookie-jar expression. "Look," he replied, "the answer to the first part of your question is 'none of your business.' To the second, let's see, oh, yeah, gold is where you find it!"

Where to Look for Gold in Vermont

Where to find gold in Vermont today. Card 7.

During the summer of 1975, gold in varying quantities was found in all of these locations in Vermont:

Rock River in Newfane and Dover
West River in Townsend and Jamaica
Williams River in Ludlow
Ottauquechee River in Bridgewater
White River in Stockbridge and Rochester
Third Branch of White River in Braintree
Mad River in Warren, Waitsfield, and Moretown
Shady Rill Brook in Wrightsville

Minister Brook in Worcester
Little River in Stowe and Waterbury
Gold Brook in Stowe
Lamoille River in Johnson
Gihon River in Eden
Missisquoi River in Lowell and Troy
Note: if you do find what you think is gold, take it to
the State Geologist's Office in Burlington, Vermont,
and have it assayed.

Now you can see why we keep yammering about those 5x8 cards. If you include on them every snippet of your research, plus input from interviews, then play your cards right; the story will literally outline itself.

On long pieces, you may end up with a couple hundred cards. Chester Krone, the prolific men's magazine writer, spreads his out on his living room floor and moves them around until he's satisfied he has them in their proper order of appearance. Sometimes this takes several hours and at least two six-packs. When he's satisfied he has them in the right sequential order, he numbers the upper right-hand corners with a red felt-tipped pen. If he figures he'll need to refer to a card more than once, he'll attach a small "suspend" tab to it that carries an alternate number. Once this is done, Chet sits behind his typewriter and pounds out his piece. His meticulously arranged cards act as his outline.

Organization is important. Even the best writing won't hide the lack of it!

8. Heads and Leads

One day I was having lunch with Jim Daley who was at that time an associate editor of *Outdoor Life*. One of Jim's responsibilities was poking through the magazine's "slush pile" of unsolicited manuscripts to select the ones that were publishable. He was, I figured, the guy who could answer a question that had long bothered me.

"Jim," I asked, "what kind of a manuscript would really make you sit up and take notice?"

"That's easy," came his reply, "One that was written in moose blood on birch bark!"

Failing your finding a dead moose in a clump of birch trees, you are going to have to rely on a headline and lively lead to fan the faint, flickering flames of interest among the editors to whom you're trying to peddle your prose. A head on a story fills exactly the same function as a headline on an advertisement—to sell. Ideally, it's written to arrest the reader's attention.

Similarly, a strong head will arrest an editor's attention as he rifles through his slush pile. Getting an editor's attention is, and always has been, Step Number One in getting a manuscript check. There are some writers, though, including a few pros, who doubt this rather obvious truth. Recently, an experienced writer told me he wasn't wasting any more time conjuring up strong heads for his stories since editors invariably rewrote them. The real-fact-of-the-matter is that this guy has never come up with a strong head in his life. It also explains, at least in part, why he collects more rejection slips than he should be collecting. If you write a strong, provocative head, you can bet your typewriter that it will stay tagged to your story, as long as it's appropriate for the magazine. Fact is, many stories have been sold on the aegis of a strong head and not much else.

The educational level and interests of the magazine's readership has a great deal to do with how you construct your head. For example, I couldn't imagine a head that *Hustler* wouldn't print. Conversely, *The New Yorker* employs what could best be termed non-heads, which are simple, austere story headings. The editorial intent and content of these two publications are light years apart. Larry Flynt admits he edits *Hustler* to shock and titillate his readers. William Shawn, who admits to very little, edits *The New Yorker* to entertain, enlighten, and educate his audience. While *Hustler* stories are larded with four-letter words, *The New Yorker* hardly admits their existence. The lesson: before you write even the head for your story, check the intended magazine's contents. Even in this permissive age, one magazine's meat can be another's poison.

Getting a Head

The easiest heads to write are those of the one-word variety, but unfortunately, they went out of vogue in the last century. In the past year I've run across only two of them that I thought had much merit: "Foul!" heading a profile on Howard Cosell and "Ouch," heading a story about acupuncture.

Two-word heads are more common, but rarely can one be confected so that it will stand by itself without a subhead or kicker. "Orgy Etiquette" is one of those that might make the grade. (At least it made me read the article which wasn't all that informative.) The following are five two-word heads that get considerable assistance from subheads:

Pot Bust
Boston surgeons M. S. Aliapoulis and John Harmon have discovered that constant use of marijuana may cause gynecomastia—the development of female breasts in men.
High Office . . .
. . . a report on the widespread use of pot and pills on Capitol Hill.
Unnatural Act
"Perhaps most actors are latent homosexuals and we cover it with drink," says Richard Burton, adding, "I was once a homosexual but it didn't work."
Sitdown Strike
Here are the protest plans of the Committee to End Pay Toilets in America.
IQ Rx
Magnesium pemoline "intellect pills" may increase your learning speed and memory five times.

Attention Grabbers

As heads get longer, they have a tendency to lose their impact. (Did you ever see a soap powder with more than a one-syllable name?) To get around this shortcoming, writers employ various techniques to grab the reader's and editor's attention. One of these is the "play on words," approach. Here are examples, together with a brief synopsis of the stories they headlined:

Whale of a Tale About the Tail of a Whale.
Story concerned a boatload of fishermen whose boat was capsized by a whale's tail.
This Crumb Is No Milktoast.
Profile of R. Crumb, the famous hip cartoonist.
Dr. Spock's Baby Book Grows Up.
A review of the radical changes of content in the most recent edition of Dr. Spock's famous book.
Scientists Eat Their Words.
Story on a laboratory in Massachusetts that is on verge of developing edible newspapers and books.
It's Never Too Late to Start Living Longer
Article discusses aspects of aging that can be slowed or countered.
Same Crime, Different Sentence.
A study of the many injustices inherent in our present judicial system.
The Sweet Taste of Excess.
Article on America's use of sugar and the medical problems it causes.

Another attention-grabber is the head that takes a position diametrically opposite to what most readers believe. "Can Adultery Save Your Marriage?", "Your Right to Commit Suicide," "Don't Let Being 45 Stop You From Having Your First Baby," "Jogging Can Kill You," "Eat Your Way to Being Slender," and "Let's Abolish Dogs and Cats" are all fair examples of this opposite-stance head. It should be mentioned that some writers will sweat up a head like the foregoing and then jury-rig a story around that head. While this may be a questionable practice that often requires stretching facts to their breaking point, it does sell stories to some editors. Unfortunately, more and more of these stories that don't deliver what the head promises are being published.

Some heads are gossipy like the stories they preface. "How President's Sons Sneak Girls into the White House," "Sonny: I Want Cher Back," and "Burt Reynold's Little-Known Stretch in Jail" are firmly in this category. If you want to take a crash course in writing this type of head, thumb through the *National Enquirer, Midnight* or *The Star*.

Often, the subject matter itself makes the head work. Three surefire subjects almost always have editors sitting on the edges of their seats:

How to make money easily.
How to improve one's health and/or appearance.
How to improve one's sex life.

In the "making money easily" category, you'll find heads similar to those that follow:

"How I Made a Million While Sleeping"
"There May be a Gold Mine in Your Attic"
"Loafing Your Way to Wealth"
"Make Money on Your Vacation"
"These Lazy People Became Millionaires"
"You Don't Need Ambition to Become Rich"

Here are some from the "health and/or appearance" genre that work:

"From Slob to Sex Kitten in Six Weeks"
"Yogurt Can Add Years to Your Life"
"You Suffer More From Stress Than Germs"
"Peel Off Pounds and Enjoy It"
"Now—A Cigarette You Don't Smoke"
"A New Face for Less Than $50"
"Lose Ten Years in Ten Minutes"
"A New Cancer Drug That Works"
"From 32-28-42 to 36-24-36 Quick!"

The last of our three eye-popper categories is sex. Whether or not new sexual nostrums and techniques work, writers keep cranking stories about them out and editors kept printing them. Recent sex-related heads include:

The Extended Male Orgasm: You Can Change Your Sex Life.
From *Playboy,* this article was written in a breathless, behind-the-barn style, but revealed no information an 18-year-old wouldn't know.

P-Chlorophenylalanine—Science's First True Aphrodisiac.
What makes this insidious head a real blockbuster are the words "science's" "first" and "true." The reference to science lends immediate substance to the substance. It makes the one-word statement that it was developed by scientists in a laboratory and not by quacks in a bathtub. The word "first" implies that all previous aphrodisiacs had about the same effect on potency as a placebo. This is reinforced by the word "true." The translation here is that the stuff really works.

You can either write your head before you start writing the actual article, or wait until you're finished. Either way, there comes a time when you have to face what is to some writers the most difficult task of writing the article—settling on a lead.

A couple thousand years ago Aristotle in his *Poetics* made mention of the fact that *every* story has a beginning, a middle and an end. Things haven't changed. Your lead is your beginning. It can consist of a single sentence, a paragraph, or several paragraphs depending on the type of story you're writing, and the audience to which you're directing it. Readers of *The New Yorker,* for example, expect—indeed, almost demand—the writer start his story in some remote area far removed from his actual subject. As the writer wanders in seemingly aimless fashion, the *New Yorker* reader continues on, hoping to discern the subject of the story before the writer finally arrives at it. *New Yorker* writers have been playing this game with their readers for more than 50 years, but I'd urge you never to play it with any other audience.

Writing the Lead

The lead tells readers what they want to know, namely, what's in the story for them. Each sentence of the lead should pull them deeper and deeper into the story, using perhaps a promise, a question or a surprise to spark their interest.

Most writers will agree; the lead is probably the toughest part of any article. Some sit in front of their typewriters racking their brains until the right opening emerges, while others dive into the story head-first, hoping to find inspiration for a lead somewhere within.

Among the easiest-to-write leads is that of a straight news story. Let's take a look at three leads for the same story, all attempting to use the familiar inverted pyramid approach. The first is from the *New York Daily News:*

> A 59-year-old mystic who claimed he was Jesus Christ and led a two-month-long prayer vigil in an attempt to bring a dead follower back to life committed suicide yesterday by leaping from his 10th-floor bathroom window on West End Ave.

This lead hardly gets a passing grade insofar as we don't learn the mystic's name until we get farther into the story. The *New York Times* did slightly better with this offering:

> Oric Bovar, the cult leader who was arrested Dec. 8 when he was found trying to revive a follower who had been dead two months, jumped to his death yesterday morning shortly before he was to appear in court on a charge of failing to report a death.

While this lead is tidier and somewhat more informative, it still rates only a C+ because of dullness. Now let's go to the head of the class and see what some unsung deskman at the Associated Press did:

> Oric Bovar, the cult leader who loved cashmere and claimed he was Christ, was to stand trial Thursday for trying to raise a corpse. Instead, he jumped out a window to his death.

The bit about cashmere is a nice touch. It tells us something about Bovar. This, plus the terse last sentence and the paradox it implies, rates a solid A.

The Anecdote/Incident

Using an anecdote or incident as a lead can often hook the reader and, equally important, get the writer into the subject of a news story quickly and gracefully. Here's one from *Newsweek:*

> At a recent party in Sausalito, the young artist-host greeted his guests with the usual cheap California wine and a few joints of marijuana. But over in a corner of the room three of his friends were soon into something different. A young woman pulled a small plastic vial of fine white powder from her purse and one of her two male companions smelled the powder approvingly. The woman carefully placed six small mounds of the powder on her hand with a tiny silver spoon while the men rolled crisp dollar bills into slim straws. Then all three of them snorted the powder into their nostrils with quick expert sniffs and sat back to watch the party with grins of sudden euphoria.

This lead made it easy for the writer to get into the guts of his piece, which was about the growing use of cocaine in the United States.

Another lead that makes good use of an anecdote is Aaron Latham's opening paragraph from "National Velveeta," a story about Liz Taylor from the November '77 issue of *Esquire*. In this lead, Latham deftly uses an anecdote to bring the reader up-to-date on today's Liz.

> It was lunchtime and Elizabeth Taylor passed the salad. Once, years ago, when she was greener in judgment, Hollywood's Cleopatra passed a salad with a diamond in it to astound onlookers. Elizabeth Taylor is trying to be more discreet now that her husband is running for the Senate from conservative Virginia.

The head, "National Velveeta" carries additional significance, not only because of the movie title, *National Velvet,* but also because of the article's mention of Liz's weight problem. It clicks.

Super Ham

Time was when the only pronoun you'd find in a story was the editorial "we." No more. Today the writer can stick himself right into the lead of his story and not even blush. In writing about the filming of *Jesus Christ Superstar* for *Playboy,* Nik Cohn came up with this gem of a lead which made ample use of the personal pronoun "I" and a lot of paradox:

> Thirty miles outside Jerusalem I was taken into a labyrinth of underground caves, where the apostles and their women were performing a dance routine. The atmosphere inside was rank and airless, the heat was murderous. After half an hour, half-choked by dust, I came stumbling out into the sunlight and fell asleep beneath an olive tree, dreaming of Gadarene swine. When I awoke I saw a figure perched motionless on a rock above me, a small man in a coarse white robe, with a cassette recorder pressed against his ear. For some moments he gazed blankly at the horizon, lost in the music, and then he came down slowly toward me, to crouch beside me in the dirt. His beard was silky, his eyes full of light. *"You must be Jesus,"* I said.
>
> "Sure am," he replied, and I shook his hand. We ate shriveled olives and he nodded his head in time with the songs, sandals tapping. When the Stones became suggestive in their lyrics, however, he turned the volume down.
>
> "What does it feel like?" I asked him. "I mean, to be the Son of God?"
>
> The small man considered carefully. Lizards scurried by his feet and he stared into infinity. "Outasight," he said at last. "It's really a far-out trip."

Incidentally, the head on the above story was "Jesus Christ Super Ham," which, while irreverent, no doubt grabbed the attention of many readers.

Conflict and the Lead

Conflict is usually tough to create in a lead, since the writer must build toward the confrontation. In a story from *New Times* about

Miami's gay rights ordinance, Frank Rose neatly solved this problem:

> Dick Shack is a theatrical agent in Miami, and he's in a bind. First there's Ruth Shack, human rights advocate, Miami Metro Commissioner and sponsor of the Dade County gay rights ordinance. Ruth is his wife. Then there's Anita Bryant, born-again Christian, songstress for Florida orange juice and leader of the crusade against those who would overturn God's moral code. Anita is his client. Dick is caught in the middle.
>
> Larry King, who is in a position to know, says Dick isn't the only one. King is a talk show host on Miami radio station WIOD, and he says the gay rights debate has been threatening all kinds of relationships lately. "I've been doing radio for 20 years," he says, "and I've never seen the public like it is on this subject. If I did five hours on this every night I'd still have the phones ringing every second. It's polarizing the city."

Rose used a microcosmic conflict in his lead that quickly carries him to the macrocosmic one in the story. And while doing this he introduces a main protagonist of the story, Anita Bryant.

Dialog

Years ago, teachers of writing adjured their students never to use dialog in the opening paragraph. This stricture though, has gone the way of white bucks. Here's a neat lead from *Time* that roundly breaks this old shibboleth:

> Daughter: Mom, can I go out?
> Mother: Sure, go enjoy yourself. Don't worry about me sitting here alone all night.
> Mother has just created a classic double bind, saying yes and no to her daughter at the same time. Most parents use such paradoxical commands occasionally because they are unable to resolve their conflicting feelings. That familiar behavior may seem harmless. But according to a branch of psychiatry known as family therapy, repeated double binding is ordinarily found in families that produce schizophrenics.

The Geographical Lead

Using a geographical lead to set the scene in a news story can be fraught with more than a few dangers. Unless you're careful, your lead will read much like the opening stanzas of a travel piece, which is certainly not the most desirable pace to employ in a news story. At its best, a geographical lead can be powerful by setting the scene and providing a contrast between the place and the event. Here is a masterful one from *Time* that prefaced a cover story on the Crash of two 747s in the Canary Islands:

> The sweet scent of flowers reaching their boats inspired ancient Romans and Greeks to call them "the Fortunate Islands." The refreshingly mild and breezy climate was praised by more modern travelers as "perpetual spring." But early natives of the Canary Islands, 70 miles off the northwest coast of Africa, knew better. They chose the name Pico de Teide (Peak of Hell) for the 12,200-ft. volcanic mountain that looms broodingly over Tenerife, largest of the seven major islands: the natives thought the devil lurked inside it. Last week Tenerife was about as hellish as any place on earth can get.

In the above lead, the author has successfully contrasted the beauty of "the Fortunate Islands" to the horror of a plane crash, thus creating a beginning with impact and irony. Will the reader read on? You bet he will.

Ask a Question

Asking a question in the lead is a tricky business, for the writer must employ the kind of question that causes the reader to take notice, start thinking, and above all, keep reading. Take a look at the first two paragraphs in Moira Johnston's article, "The Last 77 Seconds of Flight 981." from the November '76 issue of *Psychology Today*. In it, Johnston uses background information about her subject to lead the reader into the series of questions that will keep him reading.

> On March 3, 1974, Turkish Airlines flight 981 left Orly Airport, in Paris, heading for London. Nine minutes after takeoff, at an altitude of 12,000 feet, a rear cargo door blew out, causing decompression, the collapse of the cabin floor above, and loss of

control. Seventy-seven seconds later the crowded DC-10 jumbo
jet crashed in a forest 23 miles northeast of Paris, killing all 346
people aboard. It was the worst air disaster in aviation history.
This is the story of the last nine minutes of flight 981.

Did they know what was happening after the explosive
decompression? What did they think as the fields and buildings
that had looked like charming toyland miniatures now loomed
closer? Were they screaming, terrified, as the plane plunged to
the earth? Were they conscious when it hit? Did they feel anything? What were the special terrors of the six passengers sucked
out of the plane upon decompression?

Johnston's thought-provoking, and somewhat horrifying questions
are all answered in the body of the article. By first providing the
reader with background information about the flight, she has successfully set the stage for the probing questions that follow.

The Lead That Spans Time

Sometimes a story will present its own difficulties in writing an
effective lead. In interpretive/investigative articles, for instance, the
writer may encounter difficulties in bringing the story up-to-date—
especially when an important event that happened years ago has triggered the investigation. Thus, the lead may have to begin with a
flashback, then quickly flash forward to the present so you can hang
onto your readers.

In a *New Times* piece, Jeff Cohen and David S. Lifton moved a
story across nine years in just four sentences. Here's how they accomplished this time-warp feat:

One moment he was standing there, smiling, telling his friend
to sing "Precious Lord" at the rally that night. Then a sound: a
single, deafening roar. And, in the next instant, he was gone.
Martin Luther King was dead, slain by an assassin's bullet.

Nine years have passed since that cool April evening at the
Lorraine Motel in Memphis, eight years since an escaped convict
named James Earl Ray stood in a Tennessee courtroom and
pleaded guilty to the crime. And still the question remains: Who
slew the dreamer? Who killed Martin Luther King?

The Problem Solving Approach

Got a problem? Who doesn't? The writer who is working on a how-to article has a unique opportunity to take a problem-solving approach in his lead. Take a look at the lead employed by William Flanagan from *New York Magazine*

> So you put off doing your federal taxes until the last minute, and now you find you haven't the time to do them, you cannot get an expert to help you with them, or you can't come up with the additional capital you owe.
>
> What do you do? As they say in the army infantry school: Do *something*—even if it's wrong. Actually, you have two options (other than doing nothing.)

Flanagan addresses the reader directly, identifies the problem, then offers him a way out. It hits home—hard.

The Action Lead

When you want your reader to be caught up in the action of the story right from the start, you need to place him right in the middle of a pertinent incident in the very first sentence. The action lead arouses interest, creates a visual scene, and starts the story off with a bang. In his lead for an *Outdoor Life* article, Erwin Bauer's anecdotal lead supplies plenty of action—in the middle of a lake.

> One morning toward the tag end of last September, Ruel Stayner slipped into a pair of rubber waders, spade-shaped scuba flippers, a slicker, and a doughnut-shaped girdle. Resembling some antennaed invader from a faraway planet, he half disappeared into the cold water of Magic Reservoir in South-central Idaho. A few moments later he was floating 100 feet or so from shore where his effortless casting betrayed an expert fly-fisherman in action. After one long cast fell softly to the surface, Ruel allowed his brown streamer fly, which imitated a leech, to sink before beginning a slow retrieve. Then he turned toward where I watched from shore.
>
> "Come on in," he shouted. Before I could answer, Ruel raised

his rod tip sharply and a second later a silvery trout jumped high
out of the lake.

Yup, this is a "how to" yarn and though you may not have guessed
it, the story concerns itself with how to use some new-fangled doug-
nut-shaped floats that will get a fisherman out into a lake or river
without a boat.

The Introductory Lead

Sometimes it is necessary in the lead to introduce someone or
something to the reader. Look at the head, subhead and lead on this
article by Sam Merrill that ran in *New Times* and pay attention to
how they work together in introducing a virtual unknown to the
reader.

Ron Laird: A Walking Disaster

*Twenty years of triumph have brought
the U.S.'s most decorated amateur
athlete proverty, homelessness and
anonymity. But he keeps on struttin'.*

Ron Laird is an amateur athlete from the United States. That's
why you've never heard of him.

Yes, I know, you've heard of a lot of American amateurs:
Mark Spitz, Bruce Jenner, Dorothy Hamill, Frank Shorter,
Howard Davis, Dwight Stones . . . . And if you're real cognos-
cente, you can probably name Jenni Chandler, John Naber, Ka-
thy McMillan, Scott May, Janice Merrill, John Peterson and,
who knows, maybe even a few more. But not Ron Laird. Right?

The above introductory lead addresses the reader directly and involves him in the story. It also leaves him asking himself, "Why
haven't I heard of Ron Laird?" To find out, he'll have to keep reading.

The Analogy Lead

If, for some reason, the lead of your article would have to be too dry or statistical to successfully grab the attention of the reader, you might try making an analogy between your subject and another more lively or understandable subject that is closer in touch with your readers.

It is hard for a reader to relate to the possibility of nuclear warfare, but by using the analogy of an automobile accident, Daniel Yergin created this hard-hitting lead in his article, "The Terrifying Prospect: Atomic Bombs Everywhere" in *Atlantic*.

> In an automobile accident there is the long moment before impact, when you see the other vehicle coming toward you, and you realize that a collision is imminent, and yet you cannot believe that it is going to happen. At last, you hear the sound of colliding metal, and you know that it is too late.
>
> The people of the world are at such a moment, on course for a nuclear collision. . . .

Yergin's summary on nuclear proliferation from this jumping-off point was successful. By beginning with an analogy, he undoubtedly kept reader interest at a high level.

Persuasive Leads

Articles of opinion are based on the viewpoints of those writers who write them. Skillful writers will back up their opinions with as many facts as they can muster.

Writing a lead for a theater review, dining out column, book review, or critical essay is a difficult order, for the writer must accomplish three things: he must offer an opinion, back up his opinion, and tell the reader something about the subject of the article.

Watch how John Simon, *New York Magazine*'s motion picture reviewer, does it.

> Airport '77 is a disaster movie that suffers from arrested development: It is a disaster all right, but it never quite makes it to being a movie. It concerns a privately owned Boeing 747 that has been converted into a flying clubhouse and is now conveying guests to the opening of a Florida museum by its millionaire owner. Thieves try to hijack the plane and manage to make it

plummet into the Bermuda Triangle. (If you expect a spectacular Sargasso Sea, forget it: For all the distinction of its plain, shallow waters, this Bermuda Triangle might as well be a Bahama Trapezoid.) The plane luckily turns out to be as airtight as the movie's plot is far from being; yet it is not quite watertight, a condition resembling that of the filmmakers' heads.

After dropping the boom on *Airport '77* in his lead, Simon goes on to explain why he dropped the boom. By doing this, he not only is giving the reader his opinion, but exactly how he arrived at it. And he tells the reader something about the plot of the movie at the same time.

Attention-Grabbers

There are leads, and then there are *leads*. The lead that demands attention is the one that will succeed, and as we've seen throughout this chapter, there are many ways a writer can create a striking lead. The nature of your material will dictate the best type of lead, or combination of several leads, for that particular story. Experiment, try several of them on for size, and then select the one that works best.

Jim Smith, an old managing editor of mine in my newspapering days, used to say, "Write a good lead and it'll lead you into a good story; write a poor one and you ain't going no place!"

While the grammar leaves a bit to be desired, no truer words were ever spoken to a writer.

9. Making It Through the Middle—With Style

Before we jump from the short lead into the long middle of a story, let's explore some of the elements of writing that may be a big help in getting you through the middle and to that goal of all writers—the end.

First off, let's get something straight. There is no right way or wrong way to write. Any method you use that allows you to get your story onto paper and meets the approbation of the editor is the right way. There is, however, good writing and bad writing—and that's what we're concerned with here.

As a writer with some small experience in teaching the craft, I have some uncertainty that it can actually be taught. I am, however, positive it can be learned and the first lesson for any aspiring writer is that he should keep his work simple; not juvenile, but simple. Every word that doesn't serve an important function should be excised from your writing. If a one-syllable word does the work of a three-syllable word, use it.

In writing, a writer is literally talking to his readers. He should constantly ask himself: "What am I trying to say to my readers? Will they understand what I've said?" If you're uncertain about either question you'd be well-advised to pause, do some clear, careful thinking and then rewrite.

A writer doesn't develop a style overnight any more than a painter does. He first learns to use his medium—words. The writer has an advantage over a painter because, if he is careful, even his simple, early works will find buyers. And as familiarity with his medium grows, a style is certain to evolve that will stamp his personality clearly upon his writing.

Good writing is always accomplished by writers who have confidence in themselves and their subject. It is impossible for me to imagine E. B. White, Norman Mailer, Tom Wolfe or Hunter Thompson approaching their typewriters with anything less than complete confidence. A writer—any writer—has more confidence when he writes in first person. The reason, I suspect, is that writing is a personal transaction between two people—the writer and reader. Thus, you may find your writing will be better if you use "I" "me," "we" and "us."

Unless a writer is a supreme egotist, and there are surprisingly few in the profession, it is extremely difficult for him to do this. He is continually nagged by the doubt, "Who am I to be telling others what I think or feel?"

The point is that *nobody* else thinks or feels exactly as you do. As a writer, it is both your right and responsibility to tell the reader what you think and feel as long as you do it honestly. Writing is a controlled act of ego and the sooner the writer comprehends this simple fact, the sooner he can write with confidence. Equally important, he will instill confidence and authority into what he writes.

Required Reading

A writer should be an insatiable reader of what his colleagues are writing and he should also be catholic in his approach to what he reads. The *best* writing doesn't always appear in the *best* magazines. Compiling a required reading list is somewhat silly, but were I a beginning writer, I would read all of these publications with some frequency: *The New Yorker, Harper's, The Atlantic Monthly, Saturday Review, Writer's Digest, Time, Newsweek, New Times, New York Magazine, Rolling Stone, Playboy, Esquire, Reader's Digest, People, The New York Sunday Times* and *The Wall Street Journal.*

While the foregoing list is a mixed bag, you won't miss too many of the current crop of front-rank writers if you stick with it. It also won't hurt if you exhume some of the writings of Thomas Paine, Henry Thoreau, H.L. Mencken, George Orwell, Bernard DeVoto, A. J. Liebling, and others of their caliber.

In your reading don't assume, just because a story appears in print, that it is a good story. Become critical—hypercritical. When you come across a piece that you admire and would dearly have loved to have written, study it, analyze and dissect it.

Start at the beginning of the writing process. Ask yourself questions: How did the author get his idea? How was the research performed? How much time did it take? Why was the lead constructed as it was? How does the writer prove his thesis in the middle of the story? Why did the writer choose this ending? By asking these questions and dozens of others, you will begin to learn the elements a writer must use to write an article that stands out. Additionally, you will gain some needed reassurance. You will quickly perceive that the experienced writer faces exactly the same problems as you. The difference is that he has learned the skills needed to solve them.

There are also two books you'd be well advised to read on a continuing basis. These are *Roget's Thesaurus* and a good, working dictionary, such as *Webster's New Collegiate. Roget's* is a treasure trove of synonyms that will save you countless hours in dredging up alternate words. The dictionary will give you the subtle shades of meaning that will allow you to pick the right word. The difference between the right word and the wrong word is the difference between a big bang and an inaudible whimper.

Understanding Usage

This discussion of right words and wrong words brings us into a gray area that academicians call usage. What is good usage? What is correct English? Can slang be used in good writing? Who is the final arbiter of what is good and what is bad?

If the English language would stand still for a few years, there's a possibility we might be able to come up with some reasonable answers to the above questions. But this isn't realistic, for English is one of the most lively and vibrant languages in the world today. It changes on a daily basis. New words are coined, new meanings are given to existing words, a noun can suddenly become a verb and vice versa. Foreign words sneak into our language from faraway places and new prefixes and suffixes get tacked onto words that previously stood alone.

Every group in our society makes its contribution to our language—criminals, lawyers, politicians, police, housewives, bankers, businessmen, et al. And some groups make contributions far out of proportion to their number. The so-called "counter culture" in its reaction against the establishment created a whole new vernacular. Less than a decade later many of these words are firmly implanted in the establishment's vocabulary: stash, pot, reefer, hash, headshop, trip, upper, bread, downer, rap, zonked, bummer, funky, gag, split, trash, rip-off, speed, roach, turn on, joint, bong, horse, gonzo, coke, copout, and crash are a few examples.

Our galloping technology almost, but not quite, outraces the words to adequately describe it: radar, sonar, diode, transistor, bubble memory, memory bank, hypersonic, supersonic, subsonic, lunar probe, blastoff, printout, microminiaturized, biodegradable, printed circuit, and there'll be more tomorrow.

Journalists coin many words, but their real stock in trade is changing adjectives to nouns (notables, greats); nouns to adjectives (top officials, health officials) or contorting them into adjectives (introspectful). They delight in using nouns as verbs (to host), or de-suffixing them to form a verb (emote), or fleshing them out to form verbs (beef up). These members of the Fourth Estate are continually *firing off* or *salvoing* off stories, *shouldering* their way through doorways, reporting events that are *upcoming,* getting the *whip hand* over their *famed* editors in order to get a raise *paywise.* One of the great joys that I derive from reading *Time* magazine is watching for these *ladyfingers of language* as they *snap, crackle* and *pop* from the *papyrus.*

The tenor of the times has much to do with the words we use. By the 1700s the Biblical whore and harlot had become a strumpet. With the coming of a new century, she became a jade, Cyprian or Paphian. As the age of Victoria dawned, she mutated into a scarlet woman, unfortunate woman, painted woman or fallen woman. By 1910, she had become a prostitute or streetwalker. Today, still working at the world's oldest profession and still up to the same old tricks, she's a hooker!

So, who are the judges of what words we should use and how we should use them? Lexicographers, the people who compile and edit dictionaries, try to keep our language purified, but it is, and always has been, a losing battle. The problem stems from the fact that by the time lexicographers get around to running up a new edition, a new word may already be firmly implanted into our language. Whether they decide to include or exclude the word, it will likely continue to be a part of our speech. About the only thing a lexicographer's imprimatur on a word means is that it can be legitimately employed in a game of Scrabble.

Not so many years ago, educators were powerful arbiters of English usage. They taught ironclad rules of syntax with iron fists.

Today, this is no longer true. Indeed, from my observations, it appears that some of the current crop of pedagogues are badly in need of some instruction themselves. As a consequence, the effect of teachers on usage is clearly moot.

This brings us to the final judge of usage—your editor. This is the gal or guy who makes the decision whether your words will be excised with a fast flick of a blue pencil. Some magazines—*The New Yorker*, for example—would never allow a word to appear that didn't repose comfortably in some dictionary. *High Times*, on the other hand, is so trendy that it should furnish readers with a glossary for each issue.

While there is often a time lag between when a word shows up orally and when it finally sneaks into print, if the word fills a need, you can be certain it will make the grade. It's like Samuel Johnson said, "The pen must, at length, comply with the tongue."

Workhorses of Writing

Before you get down to the nitty-gritty of writing, you should study parts of speech and literary techniques you may be using so that you will feel more at ease with your work. Learn all you can about them, and then make them work hard for you.

Connectives. Every good piece of writing has its own rhythm. It can be as slow and sedate as a Strauss waltz or as fast-paced as a Sousa march. In any case, the story's rhythm can make the piece more enjoyable for the reader and can add measurably to its meaning. In a well-written story, diverse ideas, facts, and dialog merge smoothly into sentences and, in turn, become paragraphs whose sequential relationship moves the story from its lead to its ending. What gives the story its rhythm are the connectives that glue everything together. Leave an important connective out, or use a defective one, and you'll break the rhythm, while your reader is left to poke about for your story line.

The English language has hundreds of connectives, which means you won't have to use the same one over and over again, as is the case in some languages. Here is a list of most-often-used connectives, with examples and information on how they are used:

Connective	Use	Example
and	To connect a series of words or two ideas of the same kind.	Today, our game biologists tell us there are probably more deer in Vermont than there were in the days of early settlement, **and** I believe them.
furthermore, besides, also, which means, in addition, again, what's more	To add another thought	Two husbands would be better than one. **Besides,** one could do the housework. Rover is a great watchdog. He **also** does naughty things on the lawn.
eventually, first, secondly, finally, next, then, since, meanwhile, later, afterwards, before, currently, nearly, farther away, in the distance, below, above, in front, in the middle, behind, to the right, to the left	To arrange ideas in order, time or space.	He sold guns and whiskey to the Indians. **Eventually,** he moved west and was never seen again. **First,** put a piece of paper into your typewriter. **Next,** you must think. **Finally,** you may start to write.
indeed, in fact, as a matter of fact	To connect one idea with another that reinforces it.	He was a genuine recluse. **Indeed,** his toenails grew so long he couldn't put on his shoes. Yesterday I awoke with a slight

hangover. **In fact,** I had to keep an ice pack on my head all day.

rather, but, still, however, nevertheless, yet, on the other hand	To connect two contrasting ideas	I like blondes. **But** I also like brunettes and redheads. Nobody likes mothers-in-law. **Nevertheless,** they can't be avoided unless you marry an orphan. He is 24 years old. And **yet,** he is the author of five novels and numerous magazine articles.
for example, in other words, for instance, by way of illustration, simply explained	To give illustration or explanation	Designers are making bikinis from exotic materials. **For example,** one is on the market made of heavy Saran Wrap. Dillinger was something of an artistic genius. Take, **for instance,** his carving a gun out of a potato.
consequently, as a consequence, accordingly, so, therefore	To connect an idea with one that follows from it.	She kicked me out of the house. **Consequently,** I brought her a mink stole and she let me back in. The Mouton

		Rothschild '64 upset me. **So** I got sick on the Louis XVI chair.
to be sure, of course, though	To make a limitation or exception	Everybody went to the family reunion. I, **of course,** stayed home. He said learning to use connectives was easy. I doubt it, **though.**
in short, to sum up, in brief	To sum up several ideas.	Editors say that writers are lazy. **In short,** they are recommending we work harder.

Verbs. If connectives are the verbal glue that keeps stories stuck together, then verbs are the major building blocks a writer uses to give his work strength, energy and clarity. Verbs are economical words. Not only do they express action, but they can also convey how the action was accomplished. Many verbs, by their very sound, suggest their meaning and some of them carry geographic connotations.

Let's take a look at the verb "walk," which means to move unhurriedly on foot. Even at best, this is an unexciting word. But let's consider some verbs that are almost synonymous. If the person doing the walking "rambled," his journey was probably a rather aimless one. If he "hiked," he was probably in the country. If he "marched," he was going somewhere with the military. "Parading" might mean he was walking up Fifth Avenue on Easter Sunday. If he "sauntered," he could well be an individual of dubious character. "Strolling" could mean he was with the love of his life. If he was "traipsing," he might be walking idly. "Mushing" would put him behind a dog sled tracking across the frozen Arctic wastes. If he was "moseying" about, he could be a western sheriff ferreting out clues, while "promenading" could put the same sheriff in the middle of a square dance.

Each of the above words has its own shading that can impart a different meaning when used in place of "walk" in a sentence. Never choose a verb that is only serviceable; choose one that will work hard to push your sentence and the reader forward. Always use active verbs and avoid those of the passive or neutral variety. Passive verbs and passive constructions are a certain kiss of death.

"Percival kissed her" is short, strong and direct. "She was kissed by Percival" is limp. Strong writing gets manuscript checks. Limp writing gets "Thank you for sending us your manuscript, but . . ."

Adverbs. Jim Smith, my old managing editor used to say, "Adverbs are useless as teats on a bull calf."

While this is an extreme statement, there is some merit in it. Adverbs tell us when, where, why, or how things happen. "He ran there." "She talked quietly." "He answered lamely." "He stood here." When used in this context, the adverb is doing the job for which it was intended. Unfortunately, some writers have a bad habit of using it to reinforce words that don't need any reinforcement. Don't write that the cannons boomed loudly or he clenched his fist tightly. You can't get much louder than a boom; nor can you clench your fist any other way. It's when adverbs are used in this manner that they meet Jim Smith's appraisal of them—useless!

Adjectives. Adjectives and adverbs are alike in that they reinforce other words. While adverbs reinforce verbs, adjectives and other adverbs, it is the job of the adjective to reinforce nouns. If we write, "She was a girl," we've told the reader one thing—the person's sex. By writing, "She was a pretty girl," we've told the reader a bit more. Now, with the help of a few more adjectives, we can give this lady some real dimension, "She was a pretty girl; dark, young and leggy."

There seem to be two distinct schools of thought on the use of these words. *The New Yorker* school views them pretty much like a missionary views sex before breakfast—with a jaundiced eye. The *New York Magazine* school, on the other hand, thinks that they are the greatest boon to writers since the invention of the pencil. Indeed, some of the New Journalists who toil for this magazine have been known to string adjectives into lines longer than those of junkies around a methadone clinic.

There's much good writing appearing today that uses adjectives so sparsely that when one pops from the page, it literally jolts the reader. This type of writing hews to the line that the concept is in the noun. Similarly, there are some writers who can splatter a paragraph with adjectives and evoke verbal imagery that leaves other writers envious.

I happen to be an addicted adjective user and make no apologies for it. I believe, however, that beginning writers should be cautious with regard to these words. Don't use them to decorate the page or to impress your readers with your wide-ranging vocabulary. Use them to make your writing stronger and more meaningful. Long-suffering readers have read enough about happy celebrants, doleful mourners, friendly smiles, unhappy frowns, purple mountains, frisky colts, towering skyscrapers, sleepy lagoons, placid ponds and stately matrons. Don't, please don't, add to their suffering!

Personal pronouns. We've mentioned it before, but it's worth mentioning again. Introverts don't make credible writers. Get yourself into your stories. Use of personal pronouns is a plus and not a penalty.

Qualifiers. The continued use of qualifiers in a story has the same effect as the lack of personal pronouns. It conveys the impression that the writer is unsure of himself and his subject. Talented writers have suffered from this malaise. Wolcott Gibbs, one of this century's best theater critics, sprinkled his reviews with qualifiers like "I fear," "I suspect," and "I'm afraid." While virtually all of the hundreds of reviews he wrote for *The New Yorker* were elegantly done and well-reasoned, they would have been much more effective if he'd shorn them of these ubiquitous, little qualifiers. Be positive in your writing. Crop out most of those pieces of verbal refuse that qualify what you think, what you see, or how you feel. There are dozens of them, such as "I imagine," "somewhat," "a little," "a bit," "very," "too," "pretty often," "sort of." Don't let them creep into your prose.

Contractions. Use them! Your writing will be warmer, more forceful and faster-paced if you do. There is just one form of contraction to be chary of—"I'd," "he'd" and "we'd." The reason is that they carry a double meaning. "I'd" can mean "I had" or "I would" and the reader may have to travel far into the sentence in order to learn the precise meaning.

Similes, overstatement and credibility. There's nothing like a good simile to add emphasis to a statement or inject some humor into a story. The problem with similes, though, is that too many of them are tired and frayed from overuse. Some have the habit of jumping out of a typewriter automatically: quick as a wink, sly as a fox, red as a rose, white as a sheet, happy as a lark, big as all outdoors, wiser than an owl, smooth as glass, rough as a cob. These should be avoided like a tubercular syphilitic. The beginning writer needs similes like these like Nixon needs Carl Bernstein. Don't use "dry as dust." If you're writing for *Harper's,* "drier than a Baptist wedding reception" might play. If you're scrivening for *New Times,* try "drier than a popcorn fart."

Now, a word about the use of overstatement: *Don't!*

Don't blow up incidents far beyond their actual proportions. Once in a while you can sneak one or two of these past an unwary editor, but readers will invariably catch you in the act. A letter or two to the editor will tip him off and after that everything you write for him becomes suspect. It's a risk not worth taking. If you can't tell it like it was or is; don't tell it at all.

Flashbacks and flash forwards. Many articles require that the writer work within more than a single time frame. It's not uncommon for an article to move back and forth across all three time frames—past, present and future. A "flashback" or "flash forward" and the device used to provide the motive power is, of course, the connective.

You can speed rapidly from the past, to the present and on into the future in just a few words. For example:

> In the past illegitimacy was relatively uncommon. Today, in Washington, D.C., illegitimate births outnumber legitimate ones. The future? No one is prepared to make a prediction.

Here's another lead that makes the transition from the past, into the present, returns to the past and then finally moves into the present again.

> If there is anything we Americans dread, it is growing old. We fear it because we falsely equate it with disease, pain, and death. And no wonder we have such misconceptions! Pathetically little attention has been paid in the past to aging as a biological phenomenon. Now, however, the situation is changing. Gerontology, the study of the aging process, is, at long last, becoming a

glamour area of research.

In 1974, for instance, Congress mandated the establishment of a National Institute on Aging (NIA), now in full swing. Anthropologists are busy exploring why people in the Caucasus Mountains of the Soviet Union and in the Andes Mountains of Ecuador are among the longest-lived individuals in the world. Aging courses are finally being taught in medical schools. The first chair in geriatric medicine in the United States was recently set up at Cornell Medical Center-New York Hospital in Manhattan.

Even with all this flashing back and forth the reader doesn't get lost because the simple connectives such as "past," "now," "1974," "for instance," and "recently" tell him where the story's at. There's a moral here: Leave these signposts out of your story and you're going to lose your readers, but before that happens you'll surely lose your chance at getting a manuscript check.

Making Characters Believable

Novelists can fiddle around for a hundred pages or more, slowly bringing a character to life in both physical and psychological dimensions. The nonfiction magazine writer, however, isn't afforded this luxury. He or she is lucky to have a few paragraphs in which to construct and breathe some vitality and credence into a character. Can you become a verbal Dr. Frankenstein while operating under this limitation? You can, with practice.

Your first step in *characterization* is to scrutinize the character you're prose is going to pin down and distinguish the characteristics that set him apart. Look carefully. These characteristics can be blatantly obvious or carefully hidden. You may find what you're looking for in his physical appearance, dress, speech, mannerisms, habits, lifestyle, economic status, educational background or a hundred and one other things.

If the character appears only once in your story, you've got to use some fast, broad brush strokes. If he pops in and out of your story, you've got the opportunity to keep adding color to his character each time he appears.

Either way, the tools at your disposal are active verbs, adjectives and dialog.

Dialog. A book, maybe three books, could be written on how to write dialog. Since we don't have that much space here, though, I'll point out a few simple rules that, if followed, will make it possible for you to weave effective dialog into your articles with a minimum expenditure of sweat.

Don't clutter your dialog with a carload of designations like "he said," "he replied," "she responded," "she retorted," or "she remarked." These speaker designations break up the rhythm of a dialog and should be used only when you think your reader needs help in understanding who is saying what. Equally important, you should be careful about using the neutral verbs listed above. *Use* "speaker designation verbs" that add dimension and insight into both the character doing the speaking and the action taking place. "Yelled," "muttered," "whispered," "croaked," "cackled," "whimpered," "cried," "squawked," "blabbered," "tattled," "babbled," et al., can do this. An adverb appended to them can sometimes give additional reinforcement and meaning, but be careful about those adverbs. *Don't* put words into the speaker's mouth. By the same token, don't take them out. If a speaker says "shit" that's exactly what you should write, even though your story is going to be sent to the *Baptist Herald.* If the editor wants to sanitize the verbiage, that's his responsibility, not yours.

Alliteration. These *pretty pieces of prose-poetry* can add *occasional objective ornamentation* to a *stark, somber, sterile story.* Don't use labored ones and don't use them too often—as this writer is prone to do.

Punctuation. If you don't know how to punctuate, my advice is to run, not walk, to your nearest bookstore and buy a book on grammar. Even if you're a grammarian of the first magnitude, you'll still have a problem. Every magazine has its own style and I can't recall ever seeing two of them that sprinkle commas, semicolons, colons, periods, dashes, and exclamation points in exactly the same way.

So what's the solution? Don't worry about it. Use the punctuation you've learned and let the editors do their timeless tinkering. This keeps them happy and prevents them from having the time to do more serious mischief such as hacking away at sentences and paragraphs that shouldn't be hacked.

Sentences. Early in my writing career the eminent American critic,

John Aldridge, told me I had a problem with periods. When I asked him what it was, he told me I didn't use them often enough. I took this valid bit of criticism to heart. Since that faraway day, anytime a sentence of mine runs longer than three typewritten lines, I start looking for ways to shorten it. The best way to do this, I've found, is to break a long sentence into two or three shorter ones. Most successful writers stick to short sentences. There are some, however, (Norman Mailer is one) who can manufacture sentences of considerable yardage and still keep syntax and punctuation under control.

From time to time, I've even seen comparative amateurs run up a sentence that left me startled if not shocked. Look at this one from an article on rugby by Richard Burton:

> It's difficult for me to know where to start with rugby. I come from a fanatically rugby-conscious Welsh miner's family, know so much about it, have read so much about it, have heard with delight so many massive lies and stupendous exaggerations about it and have contributed my own fair share, and five of my six brothers played it, one with some distinction, and I mean I even knew a Welsh woman from Taibach who before a home match at Aberavon would drop goals from around 40 yards with either foot to entertain the crowd, and her name, I remember, was Annie Mort and she wore sturdy shoes, the kind one reads about in books as "sensible," though the recipient of a kick from one of Annie's shoes would have been not so much sensible as insensible, and I even knew a chap called Five-Cush Cannon who won the sixth replay of a cup final (the previous five encounters having ended with the scores 0-0, 0-0, 0-0, 0-0, 0-0, including extra time) by throwing the ball over the bar from a scrum 10 yards out in a deep fog and claiming a dropped goal. And getting it.

Frankly, I find considerable merit and charm in this meandering maze. There's only one arguable point with respect to punctuation. Actually, this paragraph should have consisted of just two sentences, and not three. The period after the word goal, in the long sentence, should have been dropped and the last sentence should have been a part of the preceding one. The charm here lies in fact that Burton writes exactly like a Welshman talks. Having spent some of my formative years in Welsh pubs, I can modestly claim I'm something of an expert on the subject.

But back to the question: Short sentences or long ones? It's your choice, but your life and your writing will be less complicated if you stick to the short ones.

Paragraphs. Keep 'em short. This way they're more pleasing aesthetically and less likely to scare off readers.

Putting It All Together

That just about covers the bits and pieces that go into the writing of a magazine article. Now let's homogenize them to see how a story actually goes together and make some comments along the way.

How Do You Cure Writer's Block?

By Jerome E. Kelley

This is my original head. While not exactly inspired, it does its job simply because the article appeared in *Writer's Digest*. It's an odds-on bet that 99.99% of this magazine's readership has suffered from writer's block.

Byline. I wasn't using my *nom de plume* the day I wrote this.

Subhead. This was thrown in by the editor. Don't ask me why.

The lead. The problem is stated.

Promise to the reader.

Alliteration.

Transition to middle. There's the personal pronoun.

The middle. Flashback.

Simile.

It can be cured with one word, the old editor demonstrated. And the word isn't "Shazam," either.

Writer's block has been around for centuries. Aristotle wrote about it, and virtually all writers—from hacks to Hemingway—have suffered from it. As a matter of fact, longtime writers—like longtime malaria sufferers—face recurrences of the disease with almost resigned stoicism.

But nonfiction writers need never endure this economically debilitating malaise. The cure is quick, complete, free and has been around, overlooked and underused, since scribes started scribbling.

Like most individuals who have recovered from a serious illness, I like to regale people with accounts of my near-fatal brush with this virulent killer of creativity. Here's my story:

Twenty-five years ago and fresh out of college, I had the good luck to catch on as a reporter for a large upstate New York newspaper. I took to writing with the alacrity of a sex fiend with lumbago in a $3 massage parlor. In six months, I went from general assignments to police reporting, picking up a bagful of bylines and three pay raises along the way. Obviously, this idyllic journey couldn't go on forever. And it didn't.

Honor and Horror

One summer day I was summoned into the presence of the managing editor. Generally, when a reporter was called into Big Jim's *sanctum sanctorum,* it was for one purpose—to get his gluteus maximus masticated. I was not enthusiastic.

As I neared his desk, he peered out from under his green eyeshade and growled, "Sit!"

I sat.

Big Jim was editing galleys. The joyous way he wielded his copy pencil reminded me of a Nubian eunuch swinging his scimitar at a retreating Janissary. All the while he crooned an anthem of expletives that even today would be unprintable.

His glasses, whose lenses could have been purloined from the headlamps of a Stutz Bearcat, rested on a nose straight out of a Burpee catalog. It resembled a hybrid beefsteak tomato. His frayed necktie skewed off-center at 45 degrees, revealing a food-spattered shirt that was a work of art. Early Jackson Pollock.

He decapitated a full half-column from a galley, unhunched himself from the battered wooden desk, cocked his leonine head and spewed a diarrheic stream of tobacco juice toward a waste-paper basket. He missed.

As I watched this inspired performance, a stunning revelation struck me. Legendary managing editors, I mused, were not always legends!

"Kelley!" he squawked. "After long and deliberate thought, I've reluctantly concluded that you are the prize performer in this pride of pin-headed poltroons I presently preside over. In recognition of your truly outstanding mediocrity, I'm promoting you to Sunday feature editor."

"Sunday feature editor?" I couldn't hide my incredulity.

"Yes, dammit, Sunday feature editor! Now let me spell out the conditions of your thralldom."

Inserted by editor.

Characterization of Big Jim starts here.

There's one of those active verbs working hard.

This characterization could be criticized as being overdrawn. My rebuttal is that I was writing about one of the most colorful old SOBs you've ever met.

Another working verb.

Alliteration and a real beauty. Wish I could claim authorship for it, but these were Big Jim's actual words.

He held up his left hand and flicked out a thick finger as he delineated each point. "*One.* You will receive a munificent, but totally undeserved, increase of $20 per week in your present honorarium. *Two.* You will write three 1,200-word features each week. They will repose, in all their pristine beauty, on this desk at 4 p.m. each and every Thursday. *Three.* You will have the use of a photographer eight hours per week. *Four.* Do you have any stupid questions?"

I thought a moment. "What do you want me to write about?"

"*Write about? Write about?*" he shrieked. "Write about the creative ways baboons bare themselves, for all I care—but you make certain sure it has a local angle and interests our readers. Now get to hell out of here!"

Some editorial tampering here. This originally read, "Write about the menstrual cycle of Orangutans, for all I care, etc."

Lesson of the Lure

For about four weeks, everything went swimmingly. My prose was bright and nuggety. Then it happened. I couldn't come up with a story idea to save my asp.

Problem intensifies.

More editorial tampering. The editor was either getting sneaky or snaky. "Asp" originally read "ass" as I'm sure you are aware.

After several sleepless nights, haunting library stacks and seeking inspiration at local ginmills, my Thursday deadline arrived like the blade of a guillotine. Somehow I'd scratched out three stories. I gingerly placed these offerings on the M.E.'s altar and ran. They were as exciting as a Sunday morning in Philadelphia.

Simile and a pretty poor one.

My only chance for salvation lay in the fact that Big Jim was about to leave on his annual two-week fishing trip. I moped around the city room hoping that, in his rush to depart, he wouldn't have time to read and gag over my verbiage.

A copy boy sidled up beside me.

"Mr. Kelley," he said (did I detect a note of smug sarcasm?), "your friend, Big Jim, respectfully requests a tete-a-tete with his favorite feature editor."

Characterization of "Big Jim" continues.

As I entered his office, Big Jim was untangling a pile of fishing lures on his desk. He greeted me with unaccustomed—and unwarranted—civility.

"Hi, kid. Grab a seat. Want a snort?"

I nodded.

Big Jim fumbled a bottle of cheap whiskey and two dirty jelly glasses out of a desk drawer and poured three fat fingers into each. He hoisted his glass and chugalugged the potent potion.

Neat but not gaudy alliteration.

Leaning back comfortably, he clasped his hands behind his head and stared at me for an uncomfortable few seconds.

"Kid, those stories you handed in have a pervasive, redolent aroma about them—they stink! What's the problem?"

This part of the story could have been written in narrative form, but the use of dialog moves the story forward faster and is probably more effective.

"Simple," I said. "I can't get any decent ideas for stories."

"Well, you're not the first writer to have the problem. Had it once myself when I was your age."

Then, as if to change the subject, Big Jim rummaged through the lures on his desk. "Know what this is called?" he asked, holding up a fair-sized, silver one.

"Sure. A spoon."

"*How* do you suppose it got its name?"

I thought a moment before replying. "Don't know, but I've often wondered. Say, you know, that might make a story."

Big Jim chuckled and leaned forward. "You damn right it might make a story. Now, my scrawny scrivener, you've just had your first and last writing lesson from me, so let's recapitulate.

Another two-word alliteration.

"Whenever and wherever you hear the word *how*, perk up your ears. . . .

"If you think the answer to the question is of interest only to the person asking it, forget it! If the answer interests a lot of people and has a local angle, it's good for a newspaper feature. If the local angle is missing, don't throw it away. Chances are it may make a magazine article."

"OK, school's over. Now get out of here and go forth and forge the conscience of your race in the carriage of your Underwood. Meanwhile, I'm going to get out of this tee hee teepee and go fishing."

The careful reader can get some further insight into Big Jim from this bit of dialog. It's a paraphrase from James Joyce: "I go forth to forge the conscience of my race in the crucible of my soul."

A few weeks after Big Jim's lesson, I remembered his question about the fishing spoon. One slow afternoon, I sneaked off to the library. After pawing around for an hour or two, I got the answer. It was a natural for a magazine article. Seems the fishing spoon was invented in the 1800's by a Vermont boy with the improbable name of Julio T. Buel. One day, while boat fishing, Julio dropped one of his mother's coin silver teaspoons into the water. As he watched it gyrate to the bottom, a lunker fish swirled up and grabbed it. Julio got the message and rowed away to invent the famous lure.

Problem is solved.

Whoops! "Legged" is pure journalese.

As soon as I'd gathered this intelligence, I legged it for home and wrote my first magazine piece. *Vermont Life* snapped it up almost as fast as that big fish snapped up Mrs. Buel's teaspoon.

Remember how we flashed back 25 years right after the lead? Here's where we flash forward to the present.

Today, 25 years and a few hundred sales later, the word *how* is still working overtime for me. And I'm certain it would work just as hard for you.

Admonition to reader. Our "cure" for writer's block works, but with these qualifications. This is called honesty.

Hold it! Before you race off to prime your creative pump with *hows,* some advice is in order: To get the most from *how,* you'll need more than keen hearing. You'll need imagination and legwork.

There's some license here. "Several years" is actually about 24 years.

Several years ago, I was watching the *Mystery of Edwin Drood* on TV with a young lady of more-than-casual acquaintance. As the flick was ending, the young lady, who hadn't said a word during the performance muttered, "Curious. Very, very curious."

Dialog is stilted.

"What's so curious?" I asked.

"The ending. Charles Dickens died before he'd completed the story. *How* do you suppose Hollywood was able to come up with such a perfect ending?"

"Simple. They probably hired a high-priced Limey screenwriter to finish it."

"I doubt it. The ending is just too perfect, too Dickensian for a modern-day screenwriter to have carried off."

I let the matter drop. The next day, while I was pretty certain that there wasn't a scintilla of a story in the lady's question, I decided to track down who had appended the finale to Dickens' opus. My only reason was to demonstrate my superior intelligence to my inamorata by proving she was dead wrong.

"Scintilla" is a bad word. While its meaning is OK, it seems pretty strained used here.

To my chagrin, she was dead right! Shortly after Dickens' death, it became a literary fad to write an ending for *Mystery of Edwin Drood.* Scores of writers—including the leading mystery writer of the day, Wilkie Collins—tried their hands at it. Strangely, it wasn't a writer who carried off the laurels but an unlettered New England printer. The chap picked up the story line, brilliantly simulated Dickens' style and came up with the ending that won the critics' acclaim. How the Yankee printer accomplished this feat is a bigger and better mystery than the story itself.

While I wasn't able to prove my superior intelligence to the lady, I was able to salve my ego by selling the resulting story to *Fate Magazine.*

Avarice and Old Maids

Very frequently, I've found, the word *how* can lead into some totally unexpected marketplaces. Additionally, the question that triggers a story can be asked by an individual you are not particularly fond of. Here's a case in point:

From reading the subheads in this story, I'd bet the editor that wrote them keeps a fifth of vodka in his desk drawer.

I have a sister-in-law who is so niggardly she would make Hetty Green look like a spendthrift. About the only times she has ever spoken to me have been to ask a favor. Some time ago I was present at a family reunion where she was also in attendance. The only things she had contributed to the gathering were a gluttonous appetite and two loud-mouthed, slatternly daughters who would surely make the Pope come out four-square for birth control. Normally, I would avoid this frumpy harridan as I would pox of the Panamanian persuasion,

Here again, I could be accused of overdrawing a character, but you don't know my sister-in-law. These words hardly do her justice!

Simile and alliteration in one shot. Bingo!

but this day she caught me unawares and buttonholed me at the beer keg.

"Jerome, dahling," came her treacly simper, "your brother and I are refurnishing our home in early American. *How,* pray tell me, can we find an antique dealer who isn't a complete thief?"

I muttered something about trying the local Salvation Army Thrift Store and hastened off to join a maiden aunt in a bruising game of croquet.

Humorous overstatement.

A few days later a rather intriguing idea occurred to me. Perhaps, just perhaps, I would turn my sister-in-law's question into a story and, finally, make a buck at her expense for a change.

Note how short the paragraphs and sentences are throughout the story.

Over the next week or two I researched the article. I didn't become an overnight expert on antiques, but I did turn up a story of cupidity, double-dealing, avarice and knavery that was mind-boggling.

The article, as it turned out, was far too heavy for an antique or women's service magazine to buy. After studying *Writer's Market* for an hour or so, I took a real flyer. I sent the piece to *True* with a covering letter suggesting that they run it as one of their monthly True Crime Features. The editors bought my suggestion and my story and sent back a check for $1,000!

When my sister-in-law heard about this sale and how it had been generated, they claim her wails of anguish could be heard in Montreal.

At this point the editors deleted three other examples of how the word "how" generates stories. They claimed "space limitation" as their reason. Because *WD* pays on an-article-basis rather than per-word, I didn't sulk about this crop job.

Sometimes a mundane question will trigger another mundane question that, in turn, will trigger a blockbuster story.

Right after Russia's Sputnik had rocketed the world into the Space Age, I was interviewing one of the nation's leading aerospace scientists for *Aviation Week.* During the interview, I noticed a nearby table piled high with recruiting literature from a number of well-known companies.

"Are you looking for another job?" I asked.

"Nope," he replied, "but a lot of jobs are apparently

looking for me. Every week I receive 15 or 20 job offers. Look at all that fancy literature over there. *How* much do you suppose it costs a company involved in the aerospace industry to recruit a single engineer or scientist?"

How much, indeed? I shifted into high gear and ferreted out the facts concerning the astronomical amounts companies working on government contracts were spending to recruit technical personnel. The result of my digging ended up on the front page of the Sunday *New York Times* business section as the lead story.

This story resulted in a Congressional investigation or, at least, hastened one.

Sharks in New England?

Frequently, fads or anything else that's trendy can generate lots of *hows*. Shortly after Peter Benchley's bestseller, *Jaws,* hit the bookstalls the whole country was seemingly seized with shark mania. Because one of my longtime hobbies has been deep sea fishing, particularly shark fishing, I was barraged with questions concerning these fish.

Unfortunately, not one of the questions initiated a story and for a very sound reason. All of the stories that they might have generated had been already written.

One day I pulled into the local filling station in the small Vermont village where I live. In addition to getting my gas tank filled, I also got my fingers on the brass ring.

The gentleman who owns the filling station is not noted as a conversationalist. He is, however, an ardent fisherman. This day, as he filled my tank, he became positively loquacious.

"Read *Jaws?*" I nodded.
"Good book, huh?" I nodded again.
"Hear you fish for sharks?" I nodded a third time.
"How do you catch sharks in New England?"
Bang! That was the question I'd been waiting for.

Pretty fair dialog that accurately portrays my flinty Vermont neighbors.

That night I wrote a piece on New England shark fishing and sent it off, together with photographs, to *Yankee Magazine*. The editors were ecstatic with my handiwork. I'm sorry to report, however, that when the article came out, resort owners along the New England Coast did not share this feeling.

(End of Middle)

(End to Cum)

"Cum" is how editors write "come."

Many writers would end this article right here and there wouldn't be much wrong with it. When I arrived at this point, however, I got the idea for an ending that tied right back into the head. It's one of the best endings I've ever written and very, very simple. *How* would you write it?

10. The Not-So-Bitter End

How did you make out coming up with an ending for the article in the preceding chapter? If you found it a little rough, let me explain how I came by the one I used. It was simple. All I did was relate how I got the idea for the story and appended two simple words that often appear in tandem. Here it is:

> Oh, just one last thing. Over the years I've been asked one question far more frequently than any other: "Mr. Kelley, *how* do you cure writer's block?"
> Here's *how!*

You'll notice that the ending restates the problem on which the article was based and proves again that it can be solved. In essence, it is a simple summation that brings the story full circle. It isn't often that a story can be ended as neatly, concisely and effectively as this one. A good ending, aside from the lead, is the toughest part of the story to write. Most beginning writers don't really know where the ending of a story is, so they blithely write past it. When they do finally come to a halt, they find it difficult to construct an effective finis.

A nonfiction magazine article is like a skyscraper. Your lead is your foundation. Writing the middle is like adding floors, and the ending is the roof. If you add more floors than the foundation will support, the whole structure will topple over from its own weight. As a writer gains experience, the tendency to overwrite seems to subside and the ability to stop in the right place becomes almost instinctive. I've used the qualifier "almost" because I still have the tendency to overwrite. I'm certain many other writers experience the same problem.

So, when do you stop a story? Let's take a look at a diagram to see if we can come up with an answer. Diagrammed in its simplest form, a nonfiction magazine article looks like this:

Evidence of Proof   Thesis   Summation   End   Lead   Middle

Leads are, with few exceptions, mighty hard to overwrite. In the lead the writer hooks his reader, states his thesis, and moves quickly to prove it. Endings are rarely more than a paragraph or two long, so there's not much danger of overwriting them. The problem with overwriting, then, occurs in the middle of the story.

Writers, it seems, are uncertain creatures who have the bad habit of *overproving* their theses which, of course, leads to *overwriting*. Here's an example. In the preceding chapter we analyzed an article of mine, *How Do You Cure Writer's Block?* In proving my thesis that the word "how" can cure writer's block, the article used five actual examples of this word assisting me in generating salable story ideas. The original manuscript submitted to *Writer's Digest,* however, contained eight. So what happened? When the galley proofs were sent to me for proofreading, the editor informed me that the story had been shortened for "space limitation" reasons. He was being charitable. He'd put the blue pencil to my prose because I'd proved my point with five examples and he wasn't about to waste valuable space on what amounted to 1,000 words of verbal "overkill."

Moral: When you've proved your thesis or made your point, stop and get on with the ending. At worst, "overkill" will get you a rejection slip; at best, it will get your manuscript a heavy dose of editing.

Avoiding Nonendings

What about the actual ending? Most courses in writing and books on the subject skirt the end like O.J. Simpson. And the few times I've heard writers describe how they concoct article endings reminded me of a man describing how it feels to have a baby or a priest counseling someone on sex—they didn't really know what they were talking about. Sound strange? Well, it isn't. The reason writers can't give you a nice, pat formula for endings is because no writer arrives at the idea for an ending the same way twice. The ideas for some endings, I've found, come in a fast flash of serendipity. Others are the product of long hours of mulling and lots of writing and rewriting.

Endings come in two basic models—nonendings and endings. Let's dispose of the nonending first.

Have you ever read a story that literally petered out on you? Of course you have. You were reading along and suddenly the story stopped. You peered closely at the page to see if it was continued and found, to your chagrin, that it wasn't. It was then, and only then that you realized the story had ended somewhere in the middle. This is the nonending. The writer either couldn't come up with an ending or forgot to append one. The editor suffered a lapse by letting the writer get away with it. Strangely, nonendings seem to be enjoying some small vogue among a certain coterie of writers. It is, though, a lazy, annoying style of writing that you'd do well to avoid.

Here's an example of a nonending that appeared in *The Atlantic Monthly.*The title of this article is *Stranger in Holy Land* and it tells about the experiences of the author—Steven Reiner—in Israel.

> At the main airport terminal I am exhausted and edgy, and something about my face, my manner, arouses the suspicion of the first security officer I come to. She is a beautiful young woman, and how I wish she would smile. Instead, she scribbles a notation on my ticket and sends me to a line that is isolated from the rest. Funny, I think, they are going to make it as difficult for me to leave as they did for me to come in. Other people are scrutinized, their luggage is searched. I am what is euphemistically called "body checked." And asked why I came, what I did, who I saw. I haven't any good answers.

The problem is that while the reader never learns why the author went to Israel, he is further puzzled as to whether Reiner ever got out of the country. Could it be he's still being "body checked" in that steamy Jerusalem airport?

A nonending raises questions; a good ending answers them.

Endings come in myriad forms that defy characterization. Some types of endings, though, enjoy more favor among writers than others. The reason is that they are easier to write. One of the most popular is the summation ending where the writer attempts to tie his story together with a few words at the end. Some skillful writers can do this deftly with a real economy of words.

Tom Bethell, who toils for *Harper's,* is a past master at this style of ending. Here's one of his that tacks down the story and even adds a nice extra dimension:

> "If we are a united nation, then I can be a good President,"

Carter said at the end of his fireside chat. One has to admire his candor—and, I submit, his realism. Most Presidents would have put it the other way around.

Writing in *Reader's Digest,* Max Gunther neatly concluded a story on luck with just two sentences:

> People who are lucky are by definition those whom fortune has favored—but one reason they are favored is that they never assume they will be. They know fortune is fickle.

Frequently, the summary ending may have to run longer, but that doesn't mean that its length has to dilute its effectiveness. Here's the ending from John Simon's review of *A Star Is Born:*

> And then I realized with a gasp that this Barbra Streisand is in fact beloved above all other female stars by our moviegoing audiences; that this hypertrophic ego and bloated countenance are things people shell out money for as for no other actress; that this progressively more belligerent caterwauling can sell anything—concerts, records, movies. And I feel as if our entire society were ready to flush itself down in something even worse than a collective death wish—a collective will to live in ugliness and self-debasement.

Ouch!

There is no pat formula for summary endings as these three varied examples demonstrate. This type of ending, however, does have one unmistakable characteristic. It says *"The End"* in no uncertain terms.

Many writers, when an ending to an article eludes them, seek the answer to their dilemma in *Bartlett's Familiar Quotations.* What they look for is an appropriate quote from some long-expired pundit that will reinforce or add credence to their thesis. Unless the writer is selective about the quote he chooses, this type of ending can, as my Vermont neighbor, "Mutt" Taylor puts it, "Fall flatter 'n a 13-egg angel cake with the oven door open."

There are, however, many ways that proverbs, quotes, old saws and even song lyrics can be woven into an ending to make it more meaningful. A recent article in *High Times,* by Lynn Geller and Bill Madden explored the myth, folklore, history and supposed medicinal benefits of honey. The article didn't come to any firm conclusions and, because of this, the ending was obviously a tough one to write. Look how the authors used an old proverb to provide a way out of their dilemma:

> You too can enjoy many years of hale and hearty longevity on, according to some authorities, as little as a spoonful of honey a day. Your local natural-food store will be glad to supply you with many other encouraging facts as well. "Honey is a wonderful substance," a Persian proverb says, "though it does not help the dead." At any rate, it never killed anyone.

Sometimes a lucky writer—like Nick Thimmesch writing in *New York Magazine*—will run into a situation where his subject will provide him with the quote to end his story. This fortuitous event doesn't happen often, but here's an almost-too-perfect example:

> Not surprisingly, Moynihan feels rather good about things. "Oh, it's everything you've ever hoped for," he says of the Senate. "There's that wonderful line from Santayana's *The Last Puritan,* where the hero is realizing that he had everything life could give him except the ability to hug himself for his sheer good fortune." With that, Moynihan vigorously hugs himself, and says with obvious glee, "I am not puritan and I am hugging myself."

Old bromides can result in soggy endings. A little paraphrasing, though, can give them the needed zip to make a respectable, if not overly-exciting, finis. Jim Wright used one to bring his *New Times* article about sugar to a deft end.

> There may be no biological need for refined sugar. The substance may be linked to tooth decay, obesity, heart disease and diabetes. Yet, as the old saying goes, you can lead a person to a sugarless food, but you can't make him think.

When writers in search of an ending can't find what they're looking for in *Bartlett's,* I've a suspicion they turn on the radio. The quote they're seeking may be hidden in the lyrics of a song. If the song is an obscure one, the singer, composer or song's protagonist may require identification. Here's an ending from an article that appeared in *Harper's* that does exactly this:

> Like Sam Hall of the folk song saying, on the gallows, "I hate you one and all," Gary Gilmore represented all murderers at the moment of execution. He had made the decision to die before he committed the first murder. He no longer feared death. There was anxiety about the pain that might be connected with the physical execution of the sentence he had been allowed to set for himself, but he could not have feared death. His demand for capital punishment was no more than the articulation of the wish of every assassin. The enormous hatred that drives a man to negate the world spoke: "Let's do it." The anomic victory was his.

On the other hand, the lyrics may be so well-known that you'll only have to use a fragment to achieve the effect you are seeking, as demonstrated by this ending:

> Then, too, Brazilians don't seem dismayed by a boycott threat. Indeed, they say that any reduction of U.S. consumption will help them meet demand. Depressing as it may seem, Americans will likely have to keep on paying high prices for their favorite beverage until there is once again "an awful lot of coffee in Brazil."

When a writer tackles an investigative or round-up article whose subject portends impending disaster for the world, a country or certain individuals, it's incumbent upon him to offer suggestions on how the disaster can be averted. Under no circumstances can he leave his reader devoid of all hope. The reason? Editors won't let him. Even the most pessimistic editors I know (and I know several) will not run an article that has a *totally* downbeat ending. I'm not certain why this is so, but I suppose most editors believe it's bad for circulation. They figure if they sound too loudly like the klaxon of doom, readers will head for bomb shelters and newsstand sales will plummet.

Some while back I had lunch with an editor of long acquaintance who affirmed this theory. When I asked why magazine articles invariably carried upbeat endings, his response was, *"Reader's Digest carries the most upbeat of upbeat endings and their circulation is 14,000,000. It's simple. People buy magazines to be entertained; they don't buy them to be depressed!"*

Regardless of the reason, the writer who wants to sell his wares had better offer the reader some glimmer of hope no matter how gloomy his subject matter. To do this, he has to offer some advice or admonition in his ending.

When the writer knows who he is addressing, this can be relatively simple. Take, for example, this ending to an article by Stephen Oberbeck that appeared in *Good Housekeeping:*

> If what you want is to protect yourself and your family, don't wait for stern measures to be handed down from Washington. Start your own gun-control program and start it now. If there's a gun in your home, turn it over to local authorities. Get rid of it, before it gets rid of you.

Naturally, the advice offered here would have fallen on stone-deaf ears had it been offered in the pages of, say, *American Rifleman, Guns and Ammo* or *Sports Afield.*

When the disaster on which the article is based is about to befall a nation, the writer must aim his advice at individuals in government rather than the reader. Sometimes, rather than take the chance his prophesy will go unheeded, he broadly shotguns his admonition as in this ending by William E. Griffith from an article in *Reader's Digest:*

> Above all, Washington must measure up to its responsibilities in the Middle East, and fast. Only if our government takes prompt and decisive action can the looming oil squeeze and yet another war be averted. If nothing is done, we and the rest of the world will almost surely suffer one of the worst and most unnecessary disasters in history.

Once in a while a writer will tangle with an apocalyptic situation that is just too big and too complex for any single set of bureaucrats to defuse. When a writer finds himself playing at this sticky wicket, his invocation is directed toward all of mankind, even though the magazine's circulation is a sparse 325,000. *Par example,* this one by Daniel Yergin in *Atlantic:*

> It is a commonplace that nuclear warfare could extinguish civilized life. Yet that fact today is imbued with new urgency. While there is no way to stop proliferation, there are many things to be done that could help to manage the Second Nuclear Age. Even in sum, they may not be enough. Yet there is no choice but to try, and swiftly, when the alternative is the terrifying prospect of atomic bombs almost everywhere.

Endings like this can be more lethal than two dozen hydrogen bombs!

Sometimes the summary or wrap-up article needs a prediction or forecast to bring it to a logical, cogent conclusion. Some writers separate these forecasts from the main body of the story as David Tinnin does in this one from *Playboy:*

> Springing to their feet, the Israelis tried to catch the other terrorist. But it was too late. The plane had already taken off. At its next stop—New Delhi—the Dutchman was put under arrest.

★

> For the moment, the Israelis have checkmated Haddad's moves. But they cannot drop their guard for one moment, because he will never stop trying. Entebbe represents such a monumental failure to the terrorists that Haddad must be planning a new operation to exceed all his former spectaculars—if the Israelis do not pump him full of bullets first.

Making predictions often means that the writer may have to skate across thin factual ice. Writing in *New York Magazine,* Linda Wolfe accomplishes this tricky feat with unusual grace and adroitness by predicting very little:

Of course, no one knows for sure if the boom is really going to come or if the bust is simply going to deepen. As Charles F. Westoff, associate director of Princeton's Office of Population Research, says, "There's only one sure thing about predicting population trends and that is that whichever you predict, you're probably going to be wrong." Nevertheless, financial advisers and furriers, college presidents and congressmen, publishers and perambulator manufacturers are all nervously studying the end-of-the-year demographic figures and attempting to make sound forecasts. And perhaps all of us would be wise to do so, since it is inevitable that one way or the other, whether 1977 marks the burrowing in of the bust or the burgeoning forth of the boom, we are headed for major social changes as the population trend finally makes itself clear.

I doubt that there are many writers or editors who would argue that a quote is the most effective method ever devised for ending a profile article. If the quote is a good one, it will leave more than a temporary imprint upon the reader. Kenneth Clark, writing about Goya, came up with this one:

> Toward the end of his life, Goya left Spain—probably in reaction to the reign of King Ferdinand VII, the third, and worst, of his royal masters. At the age of 80, two years before he died, he wrote these words: "I can't see, or write or hear—I have nothing left but the will—and that I have in abundance."

Here's another potent one that was used by James Stewart-Gordon to end a piece about "Chicken" Colonel Sanders:

> When asked recently why he kept working at the same pace as ever, the Colonel snorted. "Work never hurt anyone," he said. "More people rust out than wear out. But not me. I'll be damned if I'll *ever* rust out."

Quotable Nonquotes

Sometimes a quote that could be termed a nonquote can make a telling point when used in an ending. Jon Bradshaw gives us some insight into British playwright, Tom Stoppard's, fey sense of humor with this ending.

"Are you prepared to stand by that?"
"Well, I write fiction because it's a way of making statements I can disown. And I write plays because dialogue is the most respectable way of contradicting myself."
"Not bad," said the journalist. "May I quote you on that?"
"There's no point in being quoted if one isn't going to be quotable," the playwright said.

Should an ending be hung onto a story with a pun? Why not? Here are the last three paragraphs from a review of Peter Fuller's *The Champions: A Psychoanalytic Study of the Heroes of Sport* that appeared in *Harper's.*Take a close look. John Lahr, the reviewer, begins his ending with a pun, adds another, and in the last paragraph nails down his thesis with yet a third.

Pun #1   Every dogma has its day. Psychology has replaced magic as our answer to forces we don't understand and are helpless to combat. It wants to explain everything, and those who question its pseudoscientific reasons are branded "defensive." Champions irritate the psychological spirit because the magic which makes them great is ultimately unanalyzable. Fuller, faced with this frustration, attacks his subject with analytic overkill. The specta-
Pun #2   cle of the sports epic is reduced to kitchen-shrink drama:

If the racing car is the phallus, then motor racing may be a substitute for masturbation. . . . The "coil spring/damper units," the "tubular extension" which passes over the driver's legs, "cockpits," "swinging members," and the "rubber bag fuel tanks" and their location all immediately indicate the male genitals. We can even suggest comparable functions, linking suspension with the erectile tissue; getting into gear, transmission and propulsion with erection and penile movement; exhaust with urination; lubrication with discharge of genital secretions; and winning a race with ejaculation.

Pun #3 The Champions suffer from the pathetic phallusy. Basically, Fuller is a couch quarterback, a fan who is the sophisticated extreme of the old locker room voyeur. For this athletes, not psychologists, have the right word—"pecker checker."

Old-time newspaper types often refer to "snapper" endings. The "snapper" possesses "reverse spin"—meaning the reader gets something he isn't expecting. Here's a snapper ending from a piece I wrote about amateur archaeology:

In mid-morning a boat with three scuba-equipped divers anchored a couple of hundred yards from us. Watching them for the better part of an hour it was obvious they were making a methodical search of the lake's bottom. Finally, one of them surfaced not 25 yards off our stern and curiosity got the better of me.

"Whattcha looking for?" I yelled, "Revolutionary War cannon?"

The scuba diver swam closer before he removed his mask and replied, "Naw, back in 1929-1930 a rum runner's boat coming down from Canada sank around here. We're looking for a load of Canadian Whiskey."

"Think it will still be good?" I queried.

He held out a palm full of water. "Don't know, but all the corks should still be wet!"

The old saw, "All's well that ends well," doesn't apply to magazine writing. Even though you end an article with the greatest ending ever contrived, it doesn't mean your story is ready for an editor's perusal. An unpleasant, onerous and painful task awaits you—editing and revising.

The amount of editing and revising you're going to be faced with depends, to a large degree, upon the method you've used to write your story. A few writers, for instance, dictate their stories. Erle Stanley Gardner, the creator of Perry Mason, used this method successfully. Even the toilets in his home were equipped with dictating equipment and it took a battery of four or five secretaries to keep up with his torrential flow of words. While Gardner often mentioned he dictated his stories and books, he never mentioned how many revisions were necessary once his verbiage was implanted on a piece of paper. My guess would be that it was several.

Another well-known writer who, at one point in his career, tried dictating, was Mackinlay Kantor. Kantor found it was a waste of time and effort. The extensive revisions necessitated by dictating took him longer than it would have taken to write and revise a story using more conventional methods.

Sometimes, the press of business necessitates that the writer stick to the fastest method for getting his thoughts down permanently, even though he knows there will be extensive revisions later on. Ron Nessen, press secretary to former President Ford, is an example. Late each evening, after 15 to 16 hours of work, Nessen would put onto tape the events of that particular day. This verbiage will become the grist for a number of magazine articles, and, perhaps, a book or two. Nessen's technique could be better termed verbal note-taking rather than verbal writing, though.

Winston Churchill, a prolific writer among his other accomplishments, used dictation successfully in his later years—but he had a considerable amount of help. The great statesman would dictate his first draft to a secretary, who would then hand that draft over to skilled researchers who would check out the facts—dates, place names, etc. Their revisions would be incorporated into a second draft, which was prepared by a skilled editor on Churchill's staff. This draft would be given to the great man for his final polishing.

Unfortunately, we can't all afford to employ such an able staff. Therefore, we must find the best method of writing that suits our habits, timetable, and other needs.

Most writers do their writing on typewriters. Some sit down at the keyboard, bat out a story in a couple of hours, and then spend the next couple days doing revisions. Others write much more slowly and, as a consequence, have fewer revisions awaiting them at the end of a piece. There are exceptions, though. Dan Jenkins, one of the big stars of *Sports Illustrated,* seldom takes notes and spends no more than two hours knocking out a 3,000-word story that is funny, entertaining, informative, and seldom needs *any* revisions. Needless to say, there aren't many Dan Jenkins in the writing profession.

The final method of committing a story to paper is good, old-fashioned longhand. It may come as a shock, but a surprisingly large number of writers still adhere to this arcane but effective technique for a sound reason. These writers believe that a typewriter distracts them by interposing itself between the writer and his words. A pen or pencil, they feel, doesn't do this because it is an extension of the arm. There may be considerable merit to this view because writers who use longhand do far fewer revisions than writers using the other methods. In any case, this is by far the slowest method of getting your story onto paper.

If you happen to be in a large library that has original manuscripts, you can easily verify this fact. Handwritten manuscripts usually carry less than one-third of the revisions usually found on manuscripts of the typed variety.

The Writer As Editor

Astute writers use a Jekyll and Hyde approach to the chore of revising the manuscript; the moment they finish the piece and are ready to begin revising it, they cease being the writer and become the editor. They know that the better they are at playing editor, the more stories they are going to sell.

The best way to revise and edit is to start at the beginning of the manuscript and, before you start hacking away at the copy, read the story a couple of times in its entirety.

If there are major faults in connectives, flashbacks, flash forwards, and sequence you'll quickly spot them. Fix these first. Next, read the story slowly and start strengthening individual words and sentences. Get rid of passive verb forms. Chop unnecessary adverbs and redundant adjectives. Prune out unneeded qualifiers. Slash sentences that aren't doing any work. Now give your story a close final reading and fix the punctuation.

At this point, before you type the story in final manuscript form, you may feel the urge to read it to somebody for their comments and criticism. Be careful! Back in my salad days, I had the bad habit of reading my stuff to anybody who would lend me their ears. In the process I didn't pick up much constructive criticism, but I did get some that was downright dangerous. Since that faraway day, I've learned to keep my own counsel.

Some writers are blessed by having spouses who are talented editors. Among them are Gay Talese, Irving Stone and Irving Wallace. Wallace says this about his missus: "She is simply one hell of an editor—sharp, sensitive, perceptive, ruthless and entirely on my wave length. Without her I'd have finished my books ten times sooner and had ten times fewer readers."

The thought occurs, that if you're intent on becoming a writer and are single, picking a helpmate who can wield a blue pencil may have very decided advantages.

11. Writing Wrongs

A sage observer of the passing parade once noted that doctors bury their mistakes, lawyers get theirs hung, and writers get theirs on the front page. Regardless of where the mistake finally reposes—in the ground, on the gallows or in the first edition—the miscreant can usually be in for a large load of trouble.

Doctors are beholden to their patients, lawyers to their clients, but the writer has a responsibility—a very real one—to his sources, his fellow writers, his editors, and to his readers. Serious writers take this responsibility very seriously. Unfortunately for the rest of us, not all writers are serious.

If your intention is to become a serious and responsible writer, there are guidelines you should follow that will enhance your professionalism and assist you in avoiding troubles that can damage both your reputation and your pocketbook.

Honesty and Objectivity

Early in every writer's career two basic truths about writing emerge, sometimes with shocking clarity. The first is the fact that the writer, through his words, wields an awesome power. He can, and frequently does, exert his influence on how people think, how they act, what they wear, what they eat, where they go, and how they spend their money. The second truth—a corollary of the first—is that the writer is frequently subjected to pressures, both subtle and otherwise, to tailor his writing to assist various individuals and groups in achieving their goals.

Pressures placed upon a writer to slant a story can range from a simple suggestion from an editor, to a threat upon his life. The most usual form is subtle (and sometimes not-so-subtle) bribery in cash, goods or services.

Are there times when a writer can, in good conscience, slant a story? The answer is a qualified "yes." When a writer writes a service piece or article of opinion he can slant the piece to conform to his *personal* views. In the case of the editorial writer, he slants an editorial to conform to the opinion of his employers. Readers should be aware of the fact that such articles are not always entirely objective.

Frequently, the writer who is asked by his editor to slant a story, can often carry off the task without compromising his professional honesty or objectivity. For instance, I was recently asked to do three articles slanted toward the idea that ski vacations are a much better value than winter vacations in the tropics. The outfit paying for the articles was the Vermont Ski Areas Association, which obviously had something of a vested interest. In writing the articles, I didn't have to tamper with or omit any facts to arrive at the predetermined conclusion. Because of this, I had no qualms that I had short-changed my readers when I received a generous check for my labors.

Unfortunately, some writers will tamper, bend, and omit facts to slant a story. A few of them do it for personal reasons, while some are simply obeying the edict of an editor. Others do it because of bribes.

Let's say that one day you're thumbing through a magazine and you come across a story about a new tourist resort on a Pacific atoll called Lava Lava. It's obviously a latter day Garden of Eden. Skies are blue, the waters sparkle, accommodations are cheap, the food is lucullan, beautiful people cavort on the dazzling white beaches, the smiling natives are friendly and unspoiled. As you read this beautifully written piece praising this new paradise, you can almost smell the redolent, sensuous smell of abundant bougainvillae. You've just received a flurry of manuscript checks and you're ready for a vacation. So, you pack your satchel and head for Lava Lava.

The moment you step into the tar paper shack that serves as the air terminal at Lava Lava, you know you've been had. Your vacation starts out with a bang—a big clap of thunder—it's the rainy season. The surly customs inspector drops your new Nikon, the roof of your hotel room leaks and the food is Polynesian Ho Jo. The other guests look like Sadie Thompson and her sisters while their escorts could be minor Mafia capos except they're not wearing colorless nail polish. The only things that are cavorting on the dirty, garbage-strewn beach are hermit crabs—and there are damn few of those.

So what happened? Some easy-to-get-to travel writer was whisked gratis to Lava Lava where he was put up free in the best hotel's bridal suite. On the day of his departure, the island's Tourist Commission threw a banquet and presented him with an Omega Chronometer.

Not to be outdone, the local Chamber of Commerce shoved a solid gold Dunhill lighter into his clammy claws. Result of his getting bribed? You got conned!

Here's another scenario that may be even more familiar. You're fed up with cooking. You're fed up with doing the dishes. One afternoon you riffle through the pages of the regional magazine that's circulated in your area and spot the "dining out" column. You read same. Wow! There's a rundown on a new restaurant, Le Trois Maggots. If it were in France, it would rate three stars in the *Michelin Guide* and if Escoffier were still alive, he probably couldn't get a job in the place as a dishwasher. That evening you pick up your true love and head for the gastronomic experience of your life. It's an experience all right. You wait two hours for a table and then comes the food. *Alors!* It would gag a pack of jackals. You wash it down with a Chateau de Chien '76 which the somelier told you was a "nice robust wine." He was right. It's so robust you probably couldn't give it away on skid row. Finally, you observe that the restaurant does have one endearing, little quality you've never noticed in any other restaurant—the *Maitre d'* picks his nose with his little finger.

A day or two later, as you recover from a case of galloping dysentery, you ruefully realize you've been had by a food writer with round heels.

Sometimes stories are slanted for reasons other than money. Back in the days when the Hearst publishing empire was really an empire, its king, William Randolph Hearst, had a mistress—Marion Davies. Miss Davies was a motion picture actress and according to most critics she was distinctly second or third rate. To any movie critic laboring for a Hearst newspaper or magazine though, she was the greatest actress to ever grace the silver screen. The Hearst critic that didn't invest Miss Davies with the talent of a Bernhardt was quickly pounding the pavement instead of his typewriter.

During the halcyon days of the *New York Herald Tribune,* this staunch, conservative defender of republicanism employed a columnist who was an exotic bird, to say the least. His name was Lucius Beebe and his column was called "This New York." Its style was so rococo that entire grottoes could have been constructed out of it. Beebe was a bon vivant and man about town who was well-born, well-connected, well-mannered, wealthy and generous. He was also a homosexual.

Beebe formed a "liaison" with Jerome Zerbe, another fashionable man about town and a photographer. In short order, his column was peppered with flattering references to his "friend." Finally, things got so bad that Walter Winchell, writing in the *New York Mirror,* seriously suggested that the column should be called not "This New York" but "Jerome Never Looked Lovelier."

I could go on and on spinning stories about writers who slant their words for money and other emoluments, but I think I've made my point. Most writers who do this fall fast from the grace of editors and are forced to take their talents elsewhere. Honesty in writing is like pregnancy—either you are or you aren't. If you are into writing for the long haul, you have only one real choice—honesty!

Protection of Sources

If, tomorrow morning, a law was passed that made it mandatory for writers to disclose their sources, by tomorrow afternoon 80% of all political and investigative reporting would come to a screeching halt. Within a month we'd be living within a system of government that would be markedly different than the one in which we live today. While it would still be called a democracy, it wouldn't function much like one. The populace would still be the recipients of "news" but it would be "managed" news the government wanted us to have. Stories about corruption, malfeasance, inefficiency, and stupidity in government would quickly disappear from the pages of the nation's newspapers and magazines. It is more than a little sobering to realize that if writers had to disclose their sources we would never have heard of Watergate, the Pentagon Papers, the picadillos of the CIA, the bombing of Cambodia, and a thousand other important stories.

When our founding fathers formulated our constitution, they ensured an ongoing democracy by setting up an intricate system of checks and balances between the executive, legislative and judicial branches of our government. But what ensures that these checks and balances will operate efficiently and honestly is a free press. And what gives the press its freedom is a codicil appended to the constitution called the First Amendment. One of its keystones is the protection of news sources.

For 200 years, a running battle has been fought between forces in government who would weaken and limit the First Amendment and the press who has sought to strengthen and expand it. There have been numerous court cases and many writers have gone to jail—at least briefly—for protecting a news source. This battle, unfortunately, will continue to rage into the foreseeable future.

When a writer protects a news source, he is protecting something infinitely more precious than a person's anonymity—he is doing his small part to protect freedom of the press.

Libel

Not long ago, A. E. Hotchner won a $125,000 libel award against Doubleday & Co. for its publication of *Hemingway in Spain,* written by Spanish author, Jose L. Castillo-Puche. The book characterized Hotchner as "toady," a "hypocrite," and an "exploiter" of Hemingway's reputation. In due course, this libel judgment was reversed unanimously in Manhattan by the United States Court of Appeals.

This episode brings up a question that many writers have asked themselves: "If the courts can't agree on what constitutes libel, how in hell can a working writer avoid it?"

In the law books, libel comes under the heading of defamation— which is generally defined as a word or act that detracts from another's good name or reputation. When the defamation is written and printed, it becomes libel.

Each person's reputation is a part of the possessions he carries through life. The courts look upon that reputation as if it were property—property that is entitled to protection just as a person's house, or other worldly goods are entitled to the protection of the law. In fact, the theory of libel extends far beyond the individual to protect the good name and the reputation of corporations, partnerships, associations, consumer goods (It's possible to libel a can of Campbell's soup!), and other manufactured items as well. It is a theory whose purpose is to protect reputation just as the theory of trespass is to protect land.

There are three basic requirements for a suit for libel. These requirements are: 1) defamation; 2) publication; and 3) identification.

We've already defined defamation—it's an act which would have the effect of injuring another's reputation. Publication is another simple element. It is a requirement that is satisfied as soon as the magazine containing the libelous article goes into circulation. (The plaintiff does not have to prove that the article was ever read by a single person.)

The third element in a suit for libel, identification, is more complicated. Most courts require that identification be so specific that there can be no question in the mind of the reader as to the identity of the person who claims to be libeled. This requirement is frequently an asset to writers who find themselves faced with a libel suit. It should be noted, however, that in more than a couple of instances, identification by name was not necessary.

Defenses for Libel

Let's say the fickle winds of fate blow in the wrong direction and you find yourself served with a complaint for libel.

When you get to court, you'll find yourself in a situation much different from what you expected. *You are not presumed innocent.* On the contrary, the burden is upon you to prove your innocence. The plaintiff—that SOB you wrote the naughty things about—has stated a sufficient case in that he showed the story was published and it identified him. Furthermore, he claims the story was false and caused him injury. Because you, as the writer, issued the first accusation, it is now up to you to prove that accusation.

There are four commonly-relied-upon defenses to a suit for libel. When there is more than one libelous comment contained in an article, it goes without saying that the author must prove substantial truth with respect to each libel. When the writer can prove that his comments were true, the plaintiff goes home empty-handed.

A second defense that can be offered in response to a charge of libel is that the plaintiff consented to the publication of the comments at issue. Just as in the case with the first defense of truth, consent in this case means consent which can be proven to a jury's or the judge's satisfaction in court and at trial. If an article has the potential for being labeled defamatory or libelous and the writer or publisher seeks the subject's consent, that consent should be in writing. It should be noted here that the subject's consent may be limited—that is to say, if the subject consents to the publication in a college or club magazine, he has not necessarily consented to general publication, especially where the article may lead to ridicule or mockery.

A third defense to the charge of libel is the eye-for-an-eye, tooth-for-a-tooth defense. The courts allow some latitude in responding to the criticism of others. Where the publication of defamatory matter is necessary in order to respond to comments which were themselves unjustified, then the courts will allow a limited right of self-defense. As in any other case of self-defense, it is a right which is qualified and should not be carried beyond the point of necessity.

A fourth defense can be found in the statute of limitations. The statute will usually vary from state to state, but in each jurisdiction, the plaintiff has a limited amount of time in which he can bring his complaint. If the charge is not brought within the time allowed between publication and complaint, then the action can be dismissed.

Privilege

If a magazine writer finds that he or she is confronted with the elements of libel and finds that the four defenses outlined above are of no avail, there is still hope. Besides the standard defenses to libel, the courts have carved out a number of privileges. That is to say, that under certain circumstances a comment which would normally be considered libelous is excusable. The courts have found that there are overriding social or constitutional ends which outweigh the need for protecting the individual's good name and, thus, some comments will be nonlibelous.

The principal foundation of most privileges in libel is built around the First Amendment to the United States Constitution. It has been long accepted that the purposes of the First Amendment go far beyond the simple guarantee of the right of free expression to an individual. That individual right has been granted because the authors of the Constitution and the judges who have interpreted it believe that a free and open exchange of ideas is essential to a strong and stable government. Because a vibrant and unsuppressed exchange of ideas is considered so fundamental to our form of government, the courts, and especially the Supreme Court, have held that where matters of public concern or where public figures are involved, the public's need to be well-informed outweighs the need to protect individual reputations. Criticism and commentary concerning public issues, matters, or figures is frequently not vulnerable to a libel suit, even if unjustified or unfounded.

On the other hand, the courts have recognized that unrestrained debate or discussion would serve no purpose whatsoever and would only damage the rights of the individuals involved. The purpose of encouraging a greater latitude of expression in the public arena is to enhance constructive criticism regardless of how misguided it might be. The courts quite naturally have sought to draw the circle tight enough so as to exclude maliciousness, mud-slinging, and even carelessness from the types of commentary and writing that is considered privileged.

Writers may report on the activities of government bodies or agencies and also matters of general public concern without having to worry about the possibility of a libel suit. The wide latitude given writers dealing in these areas by the court is known as the *privilege of reporting.*

There are four requirements that must be met before the *privilege of reporting* applies:

1. The article must deal with legislative, judicial, administrative or other official proceedings.
2. The article must be an accurate account of those proceedings.
3. The article must contain no statements which go beyond the scope of those proceedings and which might be libelous.
4. Except for New York, California, Georgia, Michigan, Oklahoma, Texas and Wisconsin, the writer cannot hold any actual malice.

Sen. Joseph R. McCarthy provided a good example of the privilege to report on legislative activities; his libels could be written about without fear of a libel suit because they were made during legislative hearings. The same would be true for activities before the state legislatures, city councils, boards of aldermen, and so on. If the most crooked politician in a state gets up before the general assembly and refers to the state's most prominent writer as a left-wing hatchet man, it is an event which can be written about without fear of libel and without the author being concerned about his having to prove the truth of the charge.

This same privilege extends to courtroom material. It should be noted, though, that privilege applies when a statement is made inside the court and is not stricken from the record, or when a document has been called to the attention of the court. Remember, the story cannot be published in order to defame the individual being tried. Accurate reports of statements made during the trial which may be false and libelous are, nevertheless, privileged.

The same privilege applies to material about important administrative proceedings. Administrative proceedings, however, frequently lack the safeguards of courtroom proceedings when they are being conducted pursuant to either statutory or executive authority.

In any event, any writer dealing with the subject of government activity who is confronted with a potentially false and libelous statement should ask himself if reporting the statement is clearly in the public interest. If, on balance, the interest of the public does not appear to be served by repetition of the statement, the statement should be excluded. As the rank of the public official being written about, or the level of the administrative proceeding diminishes, the statement which might be libelous should be scrutinized with increased care.

Public Figure Doctrine

In addition to material about government activity, other matters of general public interest and information about figures who are of public consequence may also be privileged.

Persons who generally fall into the above category include judges, legislators, executives, and candidates for public office. Works of art, motion pictures, TV programs, and other public projects and exhibitions are also included. Groups whose goal is to influence, such as the Ku Klux Klan, the NAACP, and the National Organization for Women are likewise subject to adverse comment. Additionally, private ventures are at times in the public arena—such as a large urban construction project—and are similarly subject to public criticism.

In *New York Times Company v. Sullivan,* the Supreme Court held that the constitution permits a public official to recover money damages for libel only when he can show that the libelous publication was both false and uttered with "actual malice—that is, with knowledge that it was false or with a reckless disregard of whether it was false or not." "Reckless disregard" the court later said in *St. Amant v. Thompson* "is not measured by whether a reasonably prudent man would have published, or would have investigated before publishing." There must be sufficient evidence to permit the conclusion that the defendant in fact entertained serious doubt as to the truth of his publication.

In what is probably the most important decision since the 1964 *New York Times* case, the Supreme Court held in June, 1971, in *Time, Inc., v. Pape* that no person—public or private—involved in a matter of public interest could collect damages for libel unless that person could prove that the publisher harbored actual malice. The court pointed out that it is difficult, if not impossible, to draw a line between public and private persons. To honor its commitment to robust debate on public issues, the court extended constitutional protection to all discussion and communication involving matters of public or general concern without regard to whether the persons involved were famous or anonymous.

The real question is: what constitutes matters of general or public concern in the view of the court? The answer is, unfortunately, unknown; only the parameters of this category have been outlined to date. Clearly, matters such as public expenditures or general elections fall within the category.

At the other end of the spectrum, the Supreme Court held, in 1976, in *Firestone v. Time, Inc.,* that the dissolution of a marriage through judicial proceedings is not the sort of public matter referred to in earlier decisions, even though marital difficulties of the very wealthy or the very influential may be of interest to some portion of the reading public. The real question the writer must answer is whether the matter he is concerned with is actually of public interest. Obscure people involved in an issue of momentous public consequence may be subject to the public figure doctrine, while the extremely famous and wealthy who are involved in a private matter such as a divorce may not be subject to the public figure doctrine.

The general rule has been that anonymous, obscure, and "private persons" do not have to prove "actual malice" in order to recover for libel. On the other hand, "public persons" *have had* to prove "actual malice." The distinction today is hazy at best and the true issue is whether the subject of the story is of real and serious public consequence and concern. If so, the actual malice standard should apply; but if the subject is not one of true public importance, then no such standard should apply.

Avoiding Libel

The final and fundamental question that writers must face and answer, then, is, "How is libel avoided?" The first rule is to check the facts and then check them again.

Besides doing a thorough and careful research job, the writer can, secondly, be familiar with the defenses and privileges surrounding libel. If his material is defamatory, the writer should ask if there is a legal defense for its publication. If he sees a clear defense, there's no problem, but if the writer sees no readily available defense, then he should not even submit the manuscript to a publisher.

There are several quick rules of thumb that a writer should keep in mind in dealing with material that might be libelous. First, canned phrases such as "it is alleged," or "it has been reported," have absolutely no defensive value. If a writer repeats the libel of another, he is going to be responsible regardless of phrases such as these. The writer who repeats another's libel must do so in a privileged fashion and not expect such meaningless phrases to save him.

If a libel is being printed with the consent of the subject, the writer should be certain to obtain that consent in writing. If material appears to be defamatory, but is essential to the writing itself, the author should avoid any identification of the subject or person involved. If the author is dealing with possibly defamatory material about a subject he considers to be in the public arena, he should ask if the public's need to know outweighs the subject's need and right to an unblemished reputation.

Where the subject matter is of public interest or concern, the author should ask if the facts are provably true. If those facts can be proven, then the author should ask if the material deals with public figures or public officials. The author should establish a reputation that demonstrates his high regard for the truth and for painstakingly searching out the facts. No author dealing with material that might be libelous should ever leave behind the taint of carelessness, sloppiness, negligence, or anything else that might suggest a disregard for the truth or leave a shadow of malicious intent. If the matter is one which is of public concern and the writer's material is within the ambit of fair comment or has been the result of a careful, tedious search for the truth and for fact, then the writer has little to worry about.

Plagiarism

At the height of her career, Dorothy Parker, the caustic wit and writer, was the subject of two Broadway plays—*Here Today* by George Oppenheimer and *Over Twenty-One* by Ruth Gordon. One day a friend ran into her in the lobby of New York's Algonquin Hotel.

"What's the matter, Dorothy?" he asked. "You're looking awfully depressed."

"I was just thinking," she replied, "if I ever wrote a play about myself, I'd be sued for plagiarism."

Some writers can joke about plagiarism, but for those few who get enmeshed in its toils, it can be anything but funny. Here's an example:

Alex Haley spent 14 years sweating, researching, and writing *Roots.* Overnight the book becomes a runaway bestseller. It's dramatized on TV, condensed by *Reader's Digest,* picked up by book clubs and printed in a dozen foreign languages. Haley becomes a millionaire. He also becomes the target of a "copyright infringement" suit.

The person doing the suing isn't a kook. Her name is Margaret Walker Alexander and she's a respected scholar who's been a quiet force in American letters for more than three decades. She also happens to be the author of *Jubilee,* a Civil War novel first published in 1966. This book has gone through 22 printings in the paperback edition, which means it's a mighty decent seller in its own right. Alexander is of the opinion that Haley has purloined material from her book.

Virtually every writer who is even moderately successful can find himself in a situation similar to Haley's. While there is no sure-fire way to avoid the accusation of plagiarism, an understanding of the law won't hurt you. Here's what plagiarism is all about in a not-so-small nutshell:

Plagiarism, much like libel, is very often the end product of laziness or carelessness on the writer's part. Once in a while, however, a professional plagiarist shows up and, for a short while, drives magazine editors crazy. Some years back, an Indiana man went into the plagiarism business on what amounted to a wholesale basis. Using ten or 11 aliases and about as many different mail drops, this tricky customer shipped out dozens of articles and stories he'd purloined from a number of publications. The only thing he bothered to change were the bylines. A surprisingly large number of magazines purchased and printed his bogus offerings. He was finally apprehended when he made the error of sending an article to the same magazine he'd cribbed it from.

Regardless of who perpetrates plagiarism, its boundaries are, again like libel, not particularly well defined. Essentially, plagiarism is theft—stealing the products of another person's pen and mind.

The legal premise of plagiarism is that a magazine article carries with it certain property rights. The magazine article is the result of the author's time, thought and energy. It is like a house in that through the author's creative effort the end product may be one of value to the general public. The law gives recognition to that value, and protects the property rights that are involved.

When you own a house, you have the right to use it, to sell it, to tear it down or, for the most part, do with it what you please. The law forbids another person from destroying that house or trespassing on the house; and as the owner, you may go to court to seek a remedy against those who injure your property.

Literary property is not significantly different. It is an intangible form of property, but the author nevertheless has clearly delineated property rights in his manuscript. The author owns the manuscript and the right to produce copies of that manuscript as well. Just as the law protects a person's land or dwelling house from trespass and theft, it similarly protects a person's writing, and those rights that accompany the writing.

At this point, two things should be noted. First, the common law offers the same protection for the products of a person's intellect as it does for any other form of personal property. Second, statutory protection is somewhat different and derives principally from copyright laws.

Though plagiarism and infringement are both essentially the theft of another person's property, albeit the production of mental labor and skill, there is a distinction between the two. The plagiarist is one who steals without the right to do so and without giving credit to the actual author. The infringer misappropriates without the authority to do so, but does not necessarily take credit for himself. The infringer can be a plagiarist or a pirate. Both the plagiarist and the pirate are thieves, but the plagiarist compounds the offense by taking credit as well for the material.

The purest example of plagiarism would be the copying of a story written by another person, with little or no change, and the addition of the plagiarist's name to the manuscript. This "pure" form of plagiarism was responsible for triggering two of the funniest rejection slips in the annals of magazine writing.

When Charles Hanson Towne was editor of *Delineator,* he received a sheaf of poems from a contributor. The covering letter dwelt at length on the long, arduous hours of creativity that had gone into confecting the poems and asked that payment be commensurate with the effort expended. Towne recognized the poems as his own and sent the "contributor" this rejection:

> This will acknowledge receipt of your verses, and to inform you that I have found them admirable. I can not praise them highly enough. Indeed, I like them so well that I wrote them myself a couple of years ago.

Back in the days when Robert H. Davis was editor of *Leslie's Magazine,* he received a manuscript from a Montana miner named Joseph Smith. The manuscript was laboriously handwritten on smudged, sweat-stained copybook paper. The name of the story was "The Luck of Roaring Camp" and was a word-for-word copy of Bret Harte's famous yarn. With tongue far into his cheek, Davis penned this note:

> Dear Mr. Smith:
> As much as I admired the story you have submitted, I am un-

able to publish it for a very peculiar reason. Many years ago I promised my old friend Bret Harte never to print The Luck of Roaring Camp by anyone else but himself.

Sincerely,
Robert H. Davis

Plagiarism doesn't always have to be "pure." In fact, sometimes there is a fine line between research and plagiarism. It is often said that copying from one book is plagiarism while copying from a dozen is research. There is some truth in this old saw.

When a writer goes to the trouble of gathering together a wide variety of sources and then carefully and discriminately picks and chooses passages and pieces together a new work and a new idea, the writer is not plagiarising. In fact, the work he produces is as fully copyrightable as the work he has relied upon. Other writers in turn can go back to the same sources and their research may produce the same or similar ideas. They, likewise, are not plagiarists. They are not, however, entitled to take a shortcut to that idea or to avoid doing the necessary spadework by copying the work of one who has already gathered the material.

By using another writer's phrase or string of words, a writer does not necessarily become a plagiarist. Sometimes the phrases are so well known or commonly used that they present no problems. On the other hand, a writer cannot avoid plagiarism by simply changing around the words of another author. By using the same story structure, the same ideas, and the same chain of thought, the writer can plagiarise just as if he had copied a work word for word. Plagiarism and piracy can occur without any identity of language.

The best measure of whether material has been plagiarised is to ask whether the effort of another author has been appropriated to an extent that it would diminish or injure the value of the original work. In deciding this question, a court usually looks to the nature and purpose of the passages and phrases which were used from the original work, the quantity of the material appropriated from the original work, the value and importance of that material to the original work, and finally, most importantly, the extent to which appropriating such materials from the original work will hinder sales or diminish the profits from the work, or would appear to the public to fulfill the object or purpose of the original work.

In some rare cases, a writer can exappropriate the works of others, admit it in print and then get away with it. Here's a classic and highly publicized example:

Pirating

Some years ago, the late Bennett Cerf, TV panelist and president of Random House, compiled a book called *Try and Stop Me*. How the pronoun "me" got into the title is something of a mystery. The volume was simply a compendium of jokes, anecdotes, puns and bon mots that had been lifted from writers and show business personalities. The basic source of raw material for the book, which quickly became a best seller, was a number of leading New York magazine and newspaper columnists such as Winchell, Lyons, Sobol, Wilson, Skolsky, Hoffman and others.

Apparently, Cerf anticipated some criticism if not out-and-out accusations of plagiarism and built his defenses accordingly. In the book's preface, he readily admitted he had read countless magazine and newspaper gossip columns and had lifted much of the material in his book from them. He justified this by writing, "I have tried to give credit whenever possible, but anecdotes are bandied about and sweep the country so quickly, that it is impossible to even discover who put a story into the public prints first, let alone find out who actually originated it."

Cerf cited the fact that columnists and people in show business were engaged in highly competitive vocations and their penchant for claiming originality was understandable. "However," he added, "it has always struck me as faintly ridiculous for them to cry, Thief! Thief! at rivals who very possibly overheard the gem in dispute at the same night club table or in the same gentlemen's room. They seem to forget that they actually create very few of the bright quips and amusing anecdotes they chronicle, and that the people who tell them their stories probably repeat them to a dozen others that very evening."

Accusations weren't long in coming. The loudest came from Leonard Lyons, star columnist of the *New York Post* who called Cerf an out-and-out pirate and cited the preface of *Try and Stop Me* as a public admission of piracy.

"To argue," wrote Lyons in one of his columns, "that it is all right to steal our stories because we didn't make them up—Cerf incidentally, brazenly put a copyright mark on his collection of stories taken from others—is as ridiculous as it would be to argue that it is all right to lift stories from John Gunther's *Inside Europe*. We spent years interviewing thousands of people in thousands of places to get this material. It is elementary that no one has the right to the fruit of our labor; no man, using only scissors and paste pot should benefit from another's eye- ear- and leg-work and devour, without permission reams of our columns."

In response to Cerf's assertion that someone might pass along the same anecdote to different people several times in the same evening, Lyons stated that his wife, Sylvia, had thought up a number of the quips in the book which Lyon, as a joke, had attributed to celebrities, and Cerf had recorded them exactly as uttered. How could Cerf explain that?

Cerf couldn't, but even so this case never went to court. Why? There's good reason to speculate that Lyon's lawyers told him he didn't have a case insofar as he couldn't prove that Cerf's book had hindered sales or diminished profits of his newspaper columns. After all, what can you do with an old newspaper except wrap fish in it?

For the most part, a writer must use a standard of reasonableness in determining the material which he will extract from the works of others. The writer must ask first, do I have a legitimate purpose for extracting this material; and second, is it fair to extract this material? If the writer is extracting material to be used as an illustration, or to be commented upon, or to be criticized, then the odds are that it is a legitimate use. On the other hand, if a writer is copying another's work simply to save himself the time, energy and effort required to go out and dig up the facts himself, or to sit down and write the material himself, then the material clearly should not be used.

Plagiarism and Copyright

Similarity or even identity of material is not the offense. If similar works were produced by independent efforts, there would be no infringement, plagiarism or piracy. Similarity is only the first element, but it quite naturally can lead to an inference of infringement. Besides the element of similarity, the new material must be shown to have been copied from the original material before any plagiarism or copyright infringement has been committed. The similarity between two works must be shown to be something more than the result of coincidence.

Any discussion concerned with the limits placed upon one writer's use of another writer's work necessarily involves a discussion of copyright law. Any writer who hopes to recover damages for what he believes to be plagiarism or infringement upon his work had better be certain the work in question has been copyrighted. For instance, *Peter Rabbit* is probably one of the most popular children's books ever written. Beatrice Potter, however, failed to obtain a copyright, and even though the sales figures for that book are phenomenal, those sales were of no benefit whatsoever to Potter.

Oliver Wendell Holmes, the well-known author and father of the distinguished Supreme Court Justice also had an expensive experience with copyrights. His famous work, *The Autocrat of the Breakfast Table,* appeared in 12 monthly installments in *The Atlantic Monthly.* For some reason, the issues of the magazine it appeared in were not copyrighted. The installments were collected into a single volume on which a copyright was obtained. The book, however, was pirated by another publisher and Holmes sued for infringement. The case was fought all the way to the Supreme Court—which found against the author. The reason for this opinion was that the original installments had not been copyrighted and had become part of the "public domain." The later copyright could not rescue it from this status. Once a work is published without protection of copyright, it is permanently in the public domain and free for anyone to use.

To ensure this does not happen to you, check prospective magazines to see if they are copyrighted *before* you submit your work. (The phrase "copyrighted by . . ." should appear near the front of the magazine—near the business information you'll normally find listed next to the table of contents.) If you find the publication is not copyrighted, don't fret.

You can copyright your work in an uncopyrighted magazine by simply requesting that the publisher print your work with the words *copyrighted by,* the date and your name affixed to it. The copyright notice should read, for example:

Copyright 1978 by John Doe

Once the work has been published with this notice, you can then fill out the proper form and return it to the copyright office with the $10 registration fee. For more detailed information on how to secure a copyright, write the Copyright Office, Library of Congress, Washington DC 20559.

A copyright in most instances protects only the content of a piece of literary work or other work of art. Titles are not protected by copyright, though they may be protected by other common law doctrines or statutes in some instances. Some titles are protected because they are trademarks, for instance. Basic theme and ideas similarly cannot be protected.

Furthermore, it might be noted that when two pieces of writing appeal to entirely different markets, the latitude allowed for reliance on the other writer's work is greater. For instance, a script writer could make greater use of the writings of a historian than could another historian. Likewise, a writer compiling a cookbook probably would not have committed plagiarism by using recipes found in biographies and other writings. Once in court, the actual proof of either plagiarism or infringement is difficult. Essentially, there are two things that must be proven. First, it must be shown that the alleged copier had access to the original material. Second, it must be demonstrated that the two writings are in fact similar. Proof of access must, obviously, rely heavily upon circumstantial evidence.

Copying alone is usually insufficient to allow damages. A significant amount of the original writing must have been copied, and copied material must be important to the original work. If each of these facts is present in a suit for infringement, there is a good chance that the defendant is going to have to pay damages.

Damages in such law suits are generally measured in two ways: the court may, in its discretion, award damages that it considers to be just; or, the court, if there are sufficient facts, may award actual damages—that is, profits which the author of the original manuscript has lost as a result of the infringement.

It is important to remember that the Federal Copyright Statute also provides for criminal penalties against the plagiarist or the pirate. Plagiarism is a misdemeanor which can be punished by imprisonment for not more than a year or a fine of not less that $100 nor more than $1,000 or both.

Any writer who does a significant amount of research, who is successful, and who is prolific, is going to be subject to accusations of plagiarism at one time or another. Second, if those accusations are going to be unfounded, the writer must take measures to protect himself. Third, any writer who is accused of plagiarism would do well to reread the material on libel and remember that it applies to the spoken word as well, under the label of slander. An unfounded accusation of plagiarism outside of court can become good grounds for a law suit on that theory.

In doing research, each writer should make it a point to take careful notes—dating and referencing each note. The amount of material that's been copied from another writer's work should be contained in the author's research notes themselves. Do your own research; and above all else, be certain not to rely upon the research of temporary assistants or office help who have no personal stake in the material. If the writer is accused of plagiarism, he would do well to consult an attorney with experience in the area of copyright law.

Fair Use

Each writer is entitled to make what the court calls "fair use" of other writers' material. A limited use of another writer's material may be made without the owner's permission. The most important thing to remember is not to borrow material which would materially reduce the demand for the original work. Where material is borrowed, credit should be given. Additionally, a writer should exercise some care in the quantity of material he borrows and the nature and value of that material to the original work. In most cases, a writer will have an instinctive, and usually accurate, feeling for what is and what is not fair use.

As a general rule of thumb, some publishers recommend that an author not reprint without permission more than one line of a poem, 25 words from a prose drama or a short prose composition, or 500 words from longer prose works. But rules like this do not always apply, since one line of a three-line poem, for example, would not fall into the boundaries of fair use.

Where borrowing from another writer's work is not used as a shortcut; where it does not simply repeat the work or ideas of the original author but in fact contributes to a new work and a new idea, is used as a step toward reaching that idea, and the excerpt is not lengthy, such a use will probably be fair.

Responsibility to Editors

Unlike many writers I know, I've always worked on the premise that editors are my friends—not enemies. Just because they've hacked chunks out of my stories, changed words, tightened and rearranged sentences, corrected my spelling and fixed my punctuation, I haven't flown into any towering rages. To the contrary, I've usually been thankful for this often necessary surgery. Long ago, I concluded that the objectives of writers and editors are basically the same. The writer writes to entertain and educate his readers. The editor edits to achieve maximum effectiveness for the writer's wares.

To establish a cordial, mutually profitable, ongoing relationship with editors, the writer must assume a few responsibilities—the basic one being honesty.

When you send a nonfiction article to an editor, that's exactly what it should be—nonfiction. Don't fool with the facts. When an editor accepts one of your articles, he is accepting it on the basis that every word in it is true. If, in writing the article, you've included something that you've been unable to verify, call it to the attention of the editor in a letter accompanying your manuscript. Don't ever get into the position where an editor discovers untruths or halftruths in one of your manuscripts and starts querying you.

Be honest about accepting assignments. Don't accept one unless you feel you are fully competent to finish it on time and to the specifications of the editor. If you do accept an assignment and, for reasons beyond your control you suddenly find you can't meet your deadline, inform your editor *immediately*. By doing this you'll give the editor time to fill the hole in his magazine your missed deadline will cause.

Finally, your responsibility to editors doesn't end when you receive the manuscript check. Frequently, you'll receive queries from the editor after the story has been purchased. Answer these queries on a same-day basis.

Remember, editors' hands are the ones that feed you. Don't bite them!

12. Getting Into Gear

As a beginning writer, you'll no doubt be bombarded with advice from teachers, friends, relatives, and fellow writers on what to write to break into print. Though these advisers are well-meaning, you must take their counsel with a grain of salt. One school, for instance, espouses the idea that the beginning writer should spend his time writing fillers. That's bunk! A filler is nothing but a paragraph or two that relates a single anecdote or incident, humorous or otherwise. It doesn't give the writer any practice in research nor does it necessitate any sustained writing. Even if you sold a couple of hundred of these items a year, including some of the $300 variety to *Reader's Digest,* this wouldn't make you a magazine writer—it would make you a filler writer. And believe me, there's a vast world of difference between the two.

There's another, larger school that believes the beginning nonfiction writer should get his feet wet by playing with certain "free forms" of prose such as letters, reminiscences and diaries. But this type of writing has an inherent danger. Would-be writers who have been exposed to this type of approach have a difficult time making the transition to the disciplined form of article writing that most magazines require. Their problem is that they can't carry a story from its beginning, through the middle, and to its end in a logical, sequential fashion. Editors complain about the "spatial, free form" writing they receive from new contributors. And if they don't like it—it's not going to be published.

What to Write?

Want to get your work published in a jiffy? Then get your you-know-what behind your typewriter and start cranking out short features of 800-1,200 words.

Regardless of whether you live in a snowbank north of Nome or along the concrete canyons of Manhattan, you'll stumble across dozens of story ideas that will fit this format if you use your eyes, ears and imagination. The length lends itself to any type of article—straight news, interpretive, opinion, how-to, roundup or profile. The brevity of it means you can knock it out in a relatively short span of time and, more importantly, you'll be learning to write with an economy of words. The market for these short features is a beauty. If your piece has a local or regional flavor, you can sell it to the magazine sections of your local or regional Sunday paper. If there are regional magazines in your area, these can also be a prime market. Don't, whatever you do, discount national magazines as potential purchasers of your handiwork.

Many magazines are now taking a serious look at the possibility of publishing separate regional editions serving different sections of the U.S. In 1977, *Sea* (owned by CBS Publications) went to four geographic editions geared to serve the needs of persons in the Western, Eastern, Southern, and Inland U.S. Each edition of the magazine contains both regional and national editorial material. Other magazines have regular regional sections, such as *Outdoor Life*'s "News of your Region" feature.

More and more magazines are buying short features—with a national or regional slant—and this includes virtually all the high paying ones. Editors, it seems, are learning that there are many interesting things going on in this country outside of Washington, New York and Hollywood.

Writing these short features is relatively easy. In the past two years I've sold 70 or 80 of them. It takes me only a couple hours to rap them out and payment has ranged from $100 to $500.

In my hometown, for instance, there's a local character who makes his living digging up old bottles. One spring day it occurred to me that he might be the makings of a pretty good regional yarn for a Sunday supplement. Here's the resulting story as it appeared in the *Boston Sunday Globe:*

Yeah, I know, the head stinks, but it's the newspaper's.

Bottlemania in Vermont
By Jerome E. Kelley

Keep those leads short if you're slanting a story toward Sunday supplements.

It's called bottlemania, bottleism, or just plain bottle collecting. Twenty years ago it was just a mild fever.

Today it is a raging disease. The center of this virulent epidemic seems to be centered in the beautiful State of Vermont.

Even the most afflicted aren't certain how it all got started. One venerable Vermont antique dealer figures it out this way:

It was this antique dealer, a friend, of mine, who actually touted me into this story.

"It started out as a collector's hobby that didn't require a lot of money or space. Then a couple of women's magazines ran articles on bottle collecting. After that the rush was on. The number of collectors grew by leaps and bounds, demand for bottles—almost any old bottle—soared, and prices skyrocketed.

In researching the piece, I tracked down one of these articles in *Family Circle*.

"Matter-of-fact," he added ruefully, "Sixteen-eighteen years ago I sold a big box of old bottles for $20. Today that same box would probably bring $2,000!"

Knowing my friend's penchant for exaggeration, the $2,000 figure may be a tiny bit high.

Bottle collectors make their acquisitions in three different ways—outright purchases from antique shops, at country auctions and digging for them. It's the latter that has made Vermont the Golconda for bottle collectors from all over the nation.

I also know a few writers who collect theirs in liquor stores.

The best digging sites are close to cellar holes of long-abandoned farmhouses. The Green Mountain State has an abundance of these. Shortly after the Civil War when the western lands were opening, hundreds of farmers in Vermont left their hillside, rock-strewn fields and moved to the rolling western prairies.

Researching this, I learned to my surprise that Vermont had a larger population just prior to the Civil War than it does today.

Back in the faraway day there weren't any trash collections or municipal dumps. As a consequence, farm families disposed of what little refuse they accumulated in a nearby ravine or gully. It is these now overgrown hidden heaps that today's bottle collectors seek with the avidity of a Galahad questing the Grail.

I must have been straining a little the day I wrote this simile. It's pure Victorian.

Recently I joined a professional bottle digger who sells his finds to antique dealers on one of his forays. It was one of those beautiful days with washed blue skies and a warm sun slanting down on the greening mountains.

We headed into the high country above Chittenden,

It took a while to get the personal pronoun in, but here it is. Incidentally, the only inducement the bottle digger needed for me to accompany him was a couple of cold six-packs.

Vermont. Our destination was a long-deserted settlement that appears on the maps of the late 1800's as New Boston. According to my mentor, the area had once contained 20-25 farms, a blacksmith shop, and a small general store. The last inhabitants had departed about 1910.

He pulled his four-wheel drive pickup off the potholed, rocky road and parked beside a fragrant, full-blooming lilac bush that was growing in front of a cellar hole.

"Let's start here. Unless I miss my guess the rubbish pile will be somewhere over there in that ravine," he said, pointing to a small depression about 100 yards away.

He took an electronic metal detector and a shovel out of the back of the pickup and we headed toward the ravine.

"If you're looking for bottles, how come you use a metal detector?" I asked.

"Simple," he replied, "the old-timers threw everything into their trash piles; tin cans, pieces of broken farm equipment, you name it. When you get a hot buzz on the detector over a fair area, you know you've found the place where they dumped their rubbish."

It took less than 10 minutes to get the "hot buzz" he was looking for. Laying down the metal detector and grabbing the shovel, he started to dig.

The first 10 or 12 shovelsful were unproductive; turning up an unidentifiable piece of rusty iron and the moldering fragments of a woman's shoe. Suddenly the digger let out a low whistle. "Well, I'll be . . . ," he said, holding up a small, light blue bottle about the size of my little finger and having a rounded bottom. "French perfume phial. Farmer musta loved his wife. Perfume was mighty expensive even in those days."

A few shovelsful later he turned up six bottles in quick succession.

"What are those?" I asked.

[margin notes:]

Had to search this out. The long-abandoned community had three different names. This, apparently, was the official one.

Actually, we searched three ravines before we found the right one.

He also made sure we took the two cold six-packs.

But not too fast. He seemed more interested in polishing off those six-packs.

There's an expletive deleted here that wouldn't play in a Sunday paper, particularly one in Boston.

"Spavin cure. Dr. B..J. Kendall's Spavin Cure. It was made right here in Vermont in Enosburg Falls."

"Farmer must have had a lot of sick horses," I allowed.

"Not necessarily. People used it on themselves for aches and sprains. They also soaked rags in the stuff and tied them around kids' necks when they got the croup. Wonder it didn't take the hide right off them. Kids musta been lots tougher in those days!"

When the bottle digger told me this one, I couldn't swallow it. Later, I checked on this with a couple of old-timers and found he was telling the truth.

The next few finds weren't very spectacular consisting of two celery salt bottles—a popular condiment in those days—a broken crock and the fragments of a broken chamber pot or, as my friend called it, "a thunder-jug."

Guilty here of putting words in the bottle digger's mouth. He'd called it a "pisspot."

Finally, he hit a veritable mother lode of bitters and so-called "rejuvenating tonic" bottles.

"Woman's medicine," the digger said.

"Judging from the number of bottles she must have been pretty sick."

"Doubt it," he replied. "Back in those days it wasn't very fashionable for a woman to drink. On the other hand, nobody got faulted for taking medicine. All that those bitters and tonics contained was a little flavoring and about 90 proof alcohol. When the going got tough, the woman of the house reached up into the cupboard, got down her bitters or tonic bottle, and fetched herself a snort. It kinda got her over the rough spots."

Checked this out and found that some of these so-called "rejuvenating tonics" were also laced with laudanum. In other words, heavy users could get hooked on both alcohol and drugs by sipping from a single bottle!

Life on a Vermont farm 100 or so years ago must have been one continuing series of "rough spots", I concluded.

As we headed down the mountain after the day's dig, I asked my friend how he thought we'd made out. He seemed a little reticent.

"Well, let's put it this way, we made a good day's pay—a very good day's pay."

"Ever strike it big—really big?" I asked.

He thought a long moment before replying. "Gotta admit I've had some mighty good days. 'Course I've had some pretty lean ones, too. But to answer your

The bottle digger admitted that some days he'd dug up $300 to $400 worth of bottles, but asked me not to mention it because of those "damned tax people". Anyway, the old bottle digger recently went to his reward and wherever he went, I'm pretty certain the IRS hasn't established an office there yet.

There's probably another story here if some writer would take the time to track it down.

In writing endings for these 800- to 1,200-word features, make sure they're short, sweet and say "The End" in no uncertain terms.

question: I've never ever really struck it rich like some people have. For example, like that lady from Massachusetts did last summer."

"What about her?" I inquired.

"Well, it seems she came up to Vermont and started digging just outside the Town of Pittsford. Must of had a darned good idea about what she was looking for. Anyway, before you can say 'Jack Robinson' she uncovered a pile of Civil War medicine bottles and whiskey bottles that would fill the back of this truck."

"What were they worth?"

"Don't know for sure but, from what I heard, I'd guess the proceeds would buy a mighty fine Cadillac."

"Do you think there are any more deposits like that lying aroung here in Vermont waiting to be dug up?" I asked.

He nodded to the sun that was just beginning to set behind the beautiful Hubbardton Mountains. "Do you think that will rise tomorrow morning?"

Nothing really difficult about that, is there? Just a simple straightforward "what someone did" story that packs considerable information and a bit of humor into a few hundred words.

Down in the Boondocks

Many writers and would-be writers who live in rural areas frequently complain that they have a tough time coming up with story ideas suitable for national media. It's my opinion that these writers need practice in developing story ideas and not a change of scenery in order to hype their production of higher-paying pieces. I've based this opinion on my own personal experience. Most years, I spend six months in my home state, Vermont, and the remaining six months in New York City, on the West Coast or on assignments that frequently carry me overseas. Strangely, I've found that story ideas come to me much faster in Vermont than any other place on the globe. I'm not certain why this is so, but perhaps it's because I have a tendency to think more clearly in a rural environment. This, mind you, is only speculation. One thing I am certain of is that my country location has never impeded me from getting story ideas that were suitable for national publications. I could give you dozens of examples, but let's take one that falls firmly into the 800- to 1,200-word feature category.

During the height of the Watergate misery, I was in Vermont grinding out a 20,000-word assignment. Even from this far vantage point, it was obvious that every freelance writer I knew in the Washington area was churning out stories about this sordid affair and editors were snapping them up, even though some of them were mighty shaky. I was envious. How could I get a piece of the action when I was so far from the eye of the storm? It wasn't hard. It dawned on me that one of Vermont's native sons was Calvin Coolidge whose moral rectitude was somewhat different than that of Richard Milhous Nixon's. I jumped into my car and headed a few miles down the road to Coolidge's old homestead looking for my story. Here's what I found:

Silent Cal's Home in a Quiet Town

Let's face it. This is a lousy head and I'm to blame.

By Jerome E. Kelley

It's a memorial to a former President, but one would hardly know it. It's not a soaring monument. It's not a massive piece of statuary, nor is it a multi-million dollar glass-facaded memorial library.

It's just a simple, little village set high in the hills above Vermont's beautiful Black River Valley, It's called Plymouth and it has changed little, if at all, in the last 100 years.

Perhaps the term village is a euphemism. Actually, it's a small hamlet that contains a church, a country Post Office that once was also a general store, a tiny cheese factory and a clutch of neat houses.

This is a "negative" lead and its intent is to pull the reader into the story by arousing his curiosity. By the time he gets to the end of it he should be asking, "What in hell is it?"

Plains, Georgia is a veritable metropolis compared to Plymouth, Vermont.

Across the road from the Post Office there's a small, historic sites sign that says:

PLYMOUTH
Calvin Coolidge's Birthplace

In the rear of his father's store, July 4, 1872, Calvin Coolidge was born. In back of the store is the church where he worshipped, and across from it, his home. Here on Aug. 3, 1923, he took the oath as President. In the village cemetery he rests with his father and son.

Aside from the almost scrubbed neatness of the little hamlet, the first thing that strikes the visitor is its isolated serenity. The quietness can almost be heard.

There are no uniformed guides or guided tours. The visitor is left to his own devices to wander and meditate about what quirk of destiny carried a shy farm boy from this rustic village to the highest office in the land.

Calvin Coolidge's climb to the pinnacle of this country's politics was accomplished one step at a time—slowly, tortuously and tenaciously. Perhaps no man has ever come to the Oval Office with a better set of credentials for governing his country and its citizens.

Before arriving at the presidency Coolidge had served as councilman, city solicitor, state representative and mayor of Northhampton, Massachusetts. Later he rose to member and president of the state senate, lieutenant-governor, governor, and finally, the vice-presidency.

Coolidge approached each of these positions as if they were the apogee of his political career and performed each one of them well. It would seem, looking back at the record, that he never scanned far political horizons for higher office. He moved ever upward simply because of excellence.

Wandering a few short yards to the simple Coolidge family homestead, we remembered how Calvin Coolidge was home on a visit when President Harding died. The oath of office was administered by his father,

By using the inscription on the sign we were able to save a couple of hundred words. Remember, when you're writing 800- to 1,200-word pieces, you've got to practice some real verbal economy.

There was no research involved in writing this piece. The day I got to Plymouth there wasn't another visitor in sight. Because of this, I was able to spend an hour or so chatting with two ladies who ran a small information booth. Virtually all of the information in this article was gotten from them. The remainder was derived from a couple of brochures they gave me.

a notary, with the aid of the family Bible and in the flickering light of a kerosene lamp.

Could it be, we speculated, that a man who takes an oath from a father, whom he respects, and in the very presence of his heritage will adhere more strictly to it? Our self-given answer was affirmative.

There's a quiet, but obvious, analogy of Coolidge and Nixon here.

A few steps up the hill is the small Coolidge cheese plant. The President's father was one of its founders. Today this modest business is operated by the President's only surviving son, John. In addition to the fact that it produces some of the best cheddar cheese in the country and proves high-quality, honest craftsmanship still survives; it amply proves two other points. The first is that Calvin Coolidge left the White House as a man of modest means and the second is that no succeeding Coolidge has traded his famous name for his livelihood or unearned largess.

Here's another. You'll recall there were questions raised about a brother of Nixon's receiving certain favors.

It may be over-simplifying a debatable point but it seems that only two types of presidents are remembered in after years as anything more than names: The first of these are those men who have held the office in stirring and perilous times. The other type is those few men who have endured because they marked their administrations with the strong stamp of their personalities.

Coolidge falls firmly into the latter category. When he acceded to the presidency he assumed an office that had been badly tarnished. In a few months Coolidge, through his own integrity, had restored real luster to the nation's highest post. He presided over a period in our history that has been variously known as the jazz age, the roaring twenties, and more recently, the age of Gatsby.

There was a temptation to mention the president who preceded Coolidge, Warren G. Harding, and his venal administration. By doing so I would have slowed the story down and added a lot of unnecessary verbiage.

It was a time when manners and morals were changing rapidly and a giddy population was more enthralled with entertainment than the work ethic.

At this point I knew I had the makings of a fair story, but where to end it?

With his impeccable honesty, humility, and incisive but homely common sense, he was the perfect counterbalance to a nation gone slightly awry. When he left office in 1929, he was respected and revered by a people who had all but forgotten the meaning of these words.

It was late afternoon as I walked to the hillside cemetery where the President, his family and forebearers are buried. The sun was slanting across the Green Mountains and robins were singing their plaintive song.

We spent several long moments contemplating the severely simple headstone whose inscription read: "Calvin Coolidge July 4, 1872—Jan. 5, 1933."

An elderly lady planting flowers on a nearby grave noticed our presence.

This is the type of information smart writers file away. Coolidge would make a great subject for a Fourth of July story.

"Afternoon!" she greeted. "Interested in the President?"

We allowed we were. "Did you know him?" I asked.

"Heavens, yes. Knew him since I was a little girl. Knew his father, too."

"What kind of a man was he?" I inquired.

She continued with her digging as she replied. "W-a-al, I suppose you could call him an 'extraordinary ordinary man.' "

While this ending seems almost too pat, I actually asked this question and the answer is exactly as the lady replied. I went on talking with her for quite a spell and got enough information from her for a couple more stories.

It's hard to imagine how three words could better describe our nation's thirtieth President.

While neither Nixon nor Watergate is mentioned, the inferences in this single story are obvious without being blatant. If it wasn't for Watergate, I'm certain that this story wouldn't have had a ghost of a chance of getting printed. But as it was, the piece appeared in the nation's largest Sunday paper, the *New York Sunday News.*

Manuscript Mechanics

Now it's time to hunker down behind that old Underwood or Woodstock and peck out that first 800- to 1,200-word manuscript. By following these simple rules you'll be able to showcase your writing in a way that will enhance its sale prospects:

Set the line-width of your typewriter at 55 characters, to ensure adequate margins. Leave at least 1 1/4 inches at the top and bottom, 1 1/4 inches on the left, and at least an inch on the right. Lest you think we're being picky about the margins, there's good reason! Aside from aesthetics, margins provide a place for editors to write their corrections, additions, instructions to printers, and sometimes luncheon appointments.

Double space *everything* in your manuscript and indent each paragraph eight to ten spaces. Use the regular double-spacing between paragraphs.

Your manuscript should have a title page. In the extreme right-hand corner, type your name and address, single spaced. Some writers put a word-count in parentheses under the address. The only time I ever do this is when the magazine to which I'm submitting the manuscript pays on a per-word basis. I figure this personal bit of accountancy keeps the publication honest. Incidentally, when I do count, I always count the "I"'s and "the"'s.

Center your title, which should be in caps, slightly above the middle of the page. Center the word "By" below the title and below this center your name. If you're intent on using a *nom de plume,* put it here instead of your real moniker. After it, put "pen name" in parentheses.

A big word of warning:

Don't garbage up your title page with fancy paper, asterisks, borders, or red type. If you want to let the editor know you're a rank amateur, this is the fastest way of doing it.

Your first page of manuscript should be typed differently than the others. Instead of starting at the top, drop down twelve lines before starting your text. There's no need to repeat the title.

Number all pages at the top center and in the extreme upper left-hand corner of every manuscript page, type your last name. This is important in putting stories back in order in the event some editor knocks over a mountainous "slush pile."

When you get to the end of your story, jump four spaces and type "The End" centered on the page. If you want to make like an old pro, type "-30-" instead. This is a holdover from the days when newspaper wire stories were transmitted by the telegraph instead of the teletype and -30- meant "end of transmission."

Never bind or staple manuscripts together. This makes editors twitchy and twitchy editors don't buy stories. Use paper clips.

Some writers are of the impression that if a manuscript contains a single smudge mark it will quickly qualify for a rejection slip.

Baloney! If this were true I'd still be waiting for my first acceptance. Manuscripts should be as nearly perfect as possible, but if you need to make a few corrections, pencil them in neatly. Don't spend your time as a typist; spend it as a writer.

If you're sending out photos with your story, code them with numbers. On prints, put the numbers on the back of them with a felt-point pen. Don't use pens of the ballpoint variety or pencils. In the case of color slides, put the numbers on the slide holder. Write your cutlines according to the numerical code on the photos and append them to the manuscript. This page should carry the title "Cutlines" at the top center.

It's a good idea to protect your photos with a stiff cardboard mailer, and to prevent scratches on slides, you should use plastic sleeves that are available at most camera stores.

Make sure you have a carbon copy or Xerox copy of your manuscript before you send it out. Make doubly sure you've enclosed a self-addressed, stamped envelope (SASE).

Before you stuff your manuscript into the mailbox, raise your eyes toward the heavens and utter a short prayer!

Now you're going to have to wait for the good news or the bad news. You'll hear from most magazines in three to six weeks, although some marginal magazines may take six months to give you the word. The word you get will come in the form of an acceptance or a rejection slip. As a beginning writer you're going to get many more of the latter than the former—so you might as well be prepared. A rejection slip isn't a death certificate and getting one is no disgrace. Every writer I've ever known has gotten them and some of us have gotten more than our fair share, or so it seems. Harry Edward Neal, who has written at least 18 books and a couple of big bagfuls of articles, sold his first submission and then collected 90 of these missives before he made his second sale. Altogether, he collected more than 200 before he started selling with any frequency.

My own experience is somewhat similar. I sold my first article and thought I was the world's greatest writer. After about 20 straight rejection slips, I changed my mind. Matter of fact, before I made my second sale, I was beginning to have some serious doubts as to whether I was ever literate.

Maybe Neal and I were both fortunate. I've heard of several writers who collected more than 100 rejection slips before they cashed their first manuscript check. So what do you do when one of these nixies flutters into your mail box? Do you crumple up the manuscript, fling it into the circular file, sell your typewriter, and take up macrame? Never!

The first thing you do, if the editor has been kind enough to tell you why your story was rejected, is to heed his advice.

The second thing you should do is sit down and read your story carefully—TWICE! Next ask yourself these questions: Is there a flaw in the story? Was the magazine it was sent to a good choice? How was the timing? The last item may be more important than you think. Remember, most monthly publications like to buy manuscripts five or six months before publication. If your story needs fixing; fix it. But, in any event, keep sending it out to those publications on the market list you've prepared from *Writer's Market*. Sooner or later, your perserverance and persistence is going to pay off; you're going to make a sale. And you'll never forget it when you do. Whether the check is for $4 or $400, it'll make you feel like it was for $4,000,000. Best of all, you'll have some monetary acknowledgment that *you are a writer*.

A word of caution. Just because you've sold an editor one story, don't inundate him with all your rejects. Send him *only* those stories that are appropriate for his publication.

As additional sales for your 800- to 1,200-word features come in, it's time to move into deeper writing waters. The next type of article you should tackle is the one running 2,500 words. This is the length that is most in demand by present-day magazines, and it's one you'll sell the most of throughout your writing career. Get good at it. If your early sales consist mostly of how-to pieces, start cobbling up news stories, investigative pieces, profiles, et al. Don't be afraid to move into new areas.

This is the only way you can learn to be a well-rounded, competent journeyman writer. Above all, keep expanding your markets. You can never have too many, no more than you can have too many manuscript checks.

As you gain practice at being a writer, you'll meet with a few happy surprises along the way. The first one is that the more you write, the easier it will be for you to get story ideas. Instead of being faced with the problem of *what* to write, you'll be faced with the dilemma of *which one* to write. Self-discipline comes slowly, but with each passing day it will become easier to sit down at the typewriter and crank in that first fresh piece of paper. As you learn to use libraries and other sources, research will no longer be onerous; it will become interesting and at times even exciting. Finally, while you may never write what you will consider to be a perfect story, you will continually gain increased satisfaction from your work.

Maybe, after all these years, I should be a cynic like those stereotyped writers you read about in novels. But I'm still idealistic and enthusiastic. Money, it seems to me, is surely necessary and I've never turned any of it down, but it is *not* one of writing's greatest rewards.

It pales into its proper insignificance when one considers that the writer has continuing opportunity to look at life much more closely than most of his fellow-men. He stands close to history as it unfolds. He meets and learns from the great, the near great, the meek, the humble, the beautiful and the damned. He has seen and understands the narrow gap that separates triumph from tragedy; greatness from ignominy. And if he is very lucky, he can one day draw upon this experience and fabricate a few words that, if heeded, can make this old world a little better place in which to live. I doubt if any other profession can offer such a lasting reward.

13. Equipment and Photographs

What other business can you get into today on an investment of $125? I can't think of a single one except writing.

All you need to start is a typewriter in reasonably good working order, a new ribbon, some decent 20-lb. bond typing paper, a supply of No. 90 9x12 envelopes, a few erasers, a box of paper clips and some stamps. For reference you'll need a decent dictionary (not a paperback), *Roget's International Thesaurus,* and the most recent annual edition of Writer's Market (Writer's Digest Books). If your grammar or punctuation is a bit rusty, there are several good paperbacks on the market that will, hopefully, assist you in curing this defect. Be a faithful user of *A Manual of Style* (The University of Chicago Press); *The Writer's Handbook,* by Allan B. Lefcowitz (Prentice-Hall); and *The Elements of Style,* by William Strunk, Jr. and E.B. White (MacMillan) and *On Writing Well,* by William Zinsser.

If you plan to do much interviewing, you will, sooner or later, need a cassette recorder. There are several models on the market that sell for around $50 and work reasonably well if they're treated gently. More rugged, reliable models sell for $150 and up. *Don't* buy a stereo recorder. They're finicky and have a bad habit of conking out when you need them most. Stick with a mono model for your interviews.

As you begin your writing career, you are going to be faced with a problem that may require another substantial investment on your part: photographs.

As you thumb through the pages of Writer's Market, you'll note that most magazines request—and sometimes require—photos with submitted articles. If you happen to be a photographer this doesn't pose a problem. But to most beginning writers, getting pictures to go with their words is a headache.

Your inability to furnish editors with photos along with your manuscripts can close more than 50% of all nonfiction markets to you. In other words, by not being able to submit quality photos, you can very well cut your potential sales in half.

Is there a solution? There are several, so let's take them one at a time.

Free Photos

If you are doing an article on a company, you won't have much of a problem getting suitable photos. Most major corporations have large public relations departments and they'll bend over backwards getting you suitable pix. Some companies, however, may demand to see the finished story—the idea being that if the article meets their approval, you'll get your photos. If it doesn't; forget them. Once in awhile, some of these companies will have the *chutzpa* to suggest you make changes in your story. What *you* do is your business. In the past, I've given such companies a succinct answer. It consists of a four-letter Anglo-Saxon word and a pronoun!

Smaller companies are somewhat easier to deal with. Assume you are writing a story for a trade journal about a small company's new product. The company, if it feels the resulting article will furnish beneficial publicity, might hire a photographer to work with you.

By far the largest repository for free photos is the United States Government. Every government agency employs platoons of public information officers as well as photographers. If they don't have a specific photograph in their voluminous files, they'll frequently make a special effort to get it for you. This, of course, assumes that the photo you're requesting isn't of some classified subject.

Here's a partial list of some of the government entities I've gotten photos from over the years: Department of Defense; NASA; U.S. Fish and Wildlife Service; Soil Conservation Service; Department of Agriculture; Bureau of Public Roads; U.S. Corps of Engineers; Federal Aviation Agency; U.S. Coast and Geodetic Survey; U.S. Maritime Commission; U.S. Weather Bureau (now the National Weather Service); National Institute of Health; U.S. Public Health Service; and the Department of Health, Education and Welfare.

From time to time, I've run into a few snags in dealing with slow-moving government agencies. When this happens, I drop a line to my congressman or one of my senators. I inform them I'm a writer who is having a difficult time extracting some photos from such and such agency.

Congressmen and senators, you'll find, are hypersensitive to requests made by writers and will quickly contact the agency in question. This has the same effect as putting turpentine on the tail-end of a mule. It makes them run like race horses!

Once in awhile a government photo can provide you with an unexpected bonanza. One day, when I was an associate editor of *Aviation Week,* a bundle of Air Force photos crossed my desk. One of them, a picture of a bunch of high-ranking officers receiving medals, caught my attention. On a table, behind the officers, were a number of missile models. I could easily identify all of them except one. Getting a high-powered magnifying glass from the art department, I scrutinized the unidentifiable one. Suddenly, it dawned on me that I was looking at a model of the highly-classified Titan missile just then going into production at The Martin Company in Denver. No photos of it had ever been released, nor was a release likely for a year or two.

For confirmation of my findings, I hustled the photo to Dave Anderton, *Aviation Week*'s engineering editor. "Titan!" Dave pronounced. The portion of the photograph showing the Titan was blown up and included in that week's issue. I might add that the U.S. Air Force was less than thrilled about my 20/20 vision.

State agencies can also be a motherlode of free graphics. I've gotten some absolutely beautiful pictures from various Fish and Game Departments, Conservation Commissions, Tourist Offices and Development Agencies. Moreover, some states will be happy to shoot pictures to *your* specifications.

For an up-to-date listing of hundreds of sources of free or almost-free photos, see the directory, *Picture Sources* (Special Libraries Assn.).

Photographers and Photographs on "Spec"

Every area has photographers. Some are real pros and others rank amateurs. The trick is to find one who is competent and who will work with you on a "spec" basis. In other words, the photographer will take the photos and will wait until you receive your manuscript check before he collects any pay for his work. If you collect a rejection slip for your efforts, the photographer, naturally, collects zip.

This approach to getting photos has distinct disadvantages, though. First off, you'll find that most competent photographers have a real aversion to working on "spec." Secondly, they're not always available when you want them and you'll have to rig your schedule to fit theirs. Finally, after a sale or two, some photographers have a tendency to get piggish and start raising their rates. It's generally their opinion that their pictures are selling your stories, and not the other way around. When a prima donna with a Pentax starts acting this way, you'd be well-advised to start looking for another photographer. By far the best way to avoid financial squabbles is to have the magazine send individual checks. If the photographer thinks he got short-changed, the onus falls on the editor and not you.

If price is no object, hire the best photographer you can find and chances are you'll get more than your money's worth. In the past I've worked with some real pros including Peter Miller who studied under Karsh of Ottawa and was a *Life* photographer. Pete is an artist who can do things with a camera that are bewildering and beautiful. Like all front rank photographers, his camera work can often make a soggy story sizzle.

Some photographers maintain extensive files of their work and, occasionally, you may turn up some suitable photos you can send out on "spec" from such sources. Make certain that the photo hasn't been used before. If there's anything that will send an editor rocketing through the roof, it's to find out that he's run a photo that has previously appeared in another publication. Whew!

Stock Photos

There are excellent sources of stock photos just waiting to be tapped by enterprising writers. The reason that they are not used more often is due to the fact that most writers are totally unaware of their existence. Here are the outstanding ones:

*Library of Congress.*If your story requires photos of a historical nature, you'll likely find what you're looking for in this giant repository. Best of all, it's cheap. The collection contains millions of prints in hundreds of categories. In addition to a vast array of Americana, reproductions of ancient engravings and illustrations are available at low cost. All photos in this collection are in the public domain and a catalog of the collection can be acquired for $1.25 from the Division of Prints and Photographs, Library of Congress, Washington DC 20525.

The National Archives. This is another excellent source, particularly for photos related to American history. It is the *prime* source for photographs concerned with governmental activities both past and present. A query as to whether photos are available will elicit a prompt response together with price. These inquiries should be sent to: Still Pictures Branch, Audio-Visual Records Division, The National Archives, Washington DC 20525.

The New York Public Library. This magnificent library maintains an extensive collection of photos and will sell prints of those items that are no longer protected by copyright. The best way to ascertain whether this collection contains what you are looking for is to pay a personal visit and discuss your requirements with one of the curators. Failing this, address your inquiries to: Curator of Photography, New York Public Library (Main Branch), New York City 10017.

Commercial Agencies. A growing number of commercial firms sell photos and prints of current and historical subjects. The problem in dealing with these organizations is that most of them charge on a sliding scale basis for a photo, depending upon its end use. For example, if your article is going to appear in an obscure journal, the cost of the accompanying photo may be modest. On the other hand, if your article appears in a mass circulation magazine, the cost may be astronomical.

If a story of yours requires a photo from one of these firms, your best bet is to let the magazine pick up the tab. Over the years, five or six of my stories have carried photos supplied by these organizations and the magazines have always footed the bill. It's a good thing they did; on at least one occasion the charge for one-time-use of a single photo was $400!

The largest and most reputable of these firms are:

Bettmann Archives, Inc., 136 E. 57th Street, New York City 10022

Black Star Publishing Co., 450 Park Avenue, S., New York City 10016

Brown Brothers, 220 W. 42nd Street, New York City 10036

Freelance Photographers' Guild, 110 W. 32nd Street, New York City 10001

Ewing Galloway, 420 Lexington Avenue, New York City 10017

Harris and Ewing, 1304 G Street, N.W., Washington DC 20005

Underwood and Underwood, 3 W. 46th Street, New York City 10036

Do It Yourself

Sooner or later, if you're into freelancing for the long haul, you are going to have to decide whether to become a photographer. It took me a long while to arrive at this decision myself and, as a consequence, it may be of some help if I relate my own experiences in this important, expensive, but highly profitable, adjunct to the writing trade.

Introduction to Photography

Many years ago when I first started to freelance, my productivity was limited to articles that didn't require photos and articles that could be illustrated with easily obtained stock photographs, or photos dredged up by some poor, benighted editorial assistant. Because of these strictures, only about one of every 20 of my story ideas got wrung through my Underwood.

So, what was my problem?

Actually it was pretty simple. I didn't own a camera, I wasn't going to buy one, I didn't know how to operate one, and I wasn't about to learn!

There were several reasons for my obstinancy. As a writer, I conjectured that any time spent dabbling in photography would blunt the fine edge of my sabre-sharp prose. Secondly, I figured a decent camera would cost a king's ransom. Finally, cameras scared hell out of me. With all their dials, buttons, knobs and lenses, I thought I'd need at least a Ph.D. in optics to load film into one of the damn things, much less take pictures with it!

For a long period of time—too long—I plied my trade as a freelance writer *sans* camera. Looking back at those not-so-halcyon years, it seems that I spent only about one-third of my time actually writing. The rest of my working hours were occupied thumbing through Writer's Market, winnowing from its pages those rare magazines that didn't require photos with submissions, or corresponding with editors telling them where to dig up photos to accompany the pristine prose I'd peddled them.

While I was making sales, the postman wasn't exactly getting calluses on his pinkies from poking manuscript checks into my mailbox. Then came a series of traumatic happenings that combined to make a photographer (perhaps picturetaker is a more apt descriptiton) out of me.

One day I received an assignment from a leading gun magazine. Back in that bygone era, my getting an assignment was about as rare as a B'nai B'rith Convention in Mecca. In spite of my great enthusiasm, it took me the better part of a week of sweaty writing to complete the article. It took a local freelance photographer just about 30 minutes to shoot the accompanying pix that I had set up for him.

When our checks arrived, the photographer's was for exactly the same amount as mine. I sent a letter to the editor that raised serious questions about his intellect, to say nothing of his ancestry. Needless to say, I haven't received, nor do I expect, any more assignments from this particular gentleman.

A few months after this ego-shattering experience I completed a story on trout fishing in Vermont that I considered to be one of my better efforts. I'd sold to several of the outdoor magazines, but the editors of one of the biggest and best-paying had, for reasons I was unable to fathom, shunned my submissions. This piece, I thought, was literally tailor-written to their specs and I shipped it off to them with more than my usual confidence.

In less than two weeks I received a letter from the head honcho of the magazine. He loved my story! He would buy my story! There was just one rub: he wanted pictures.

This posed a small problem. It was January and snow was crotch-high to a 10-foot Indian along the trout streams. Getting a freelance photographer to take pictures was obviously out of the question. For the next week or two I scurried around in a panic trying to uncover some pix. No luck.

Finally, I called the editor, told him about my predicament and suggested that he engage an artist to illustrate my story. He suggested I had more than one screw loose and not to send him any more stories unless they were accompanied by you-know-what.

Watching a $500 check literally flutter from my fingers because of a few lousy photos was a mighty sobering experience. Still, I hadn't learned.

The following spring I submitted a wildlife piece to a highly regarded publication whose name will remain anonymous for reasons that will become immediately obvious. The article was one of the few I've ever done whose writing could be honestly termed a labor of love. I'd lavished long hours of research on it, and polished and repolished every word. It was and still is, to my way of thinking, an almost flawless piece. Apparently the editors shared this opinion. They snapped up the offering and sent me a generous check.

My elation didn't subside until the magazine hit the newsstands. Upon seeing the printed piece, I could have cut my jugular with a dull spoon! The article was lavishly illustrated—but three of the eight accompanying photos were so wrong they were absolutely ludicrous.

While I had nothing to do with the photos or their selection, their inclusion with my piece had blown the story's credibility right off the printed page. Worse, it made me, the author, look like the south end of a northbound donkey!

That night, with a dollop or two of Cutty to ease my pain, I did some serious brooding and some serious thinking. In an hour or two I arrived at a not-so-startling solution to my problem. If I was going to achieve *maximum marketability* for my writings; if I was going to gain *maximum payment* for my labors; if I was going to ensure *maximum accuracy* for illustrations used with my articles—I had damn well better become a photographer, or, at the very least, a reasonable facsimile.

It would be nice to relate that I rushed off to a camera store, purchased a camera, snapped salable pictures immediately, wrote prosperously and lived happily ever after. It didn't quite happen that way. *Au contraire!*

Tools of the Trade

The first thing I did was subscribe to the two leading photography magazines—*Modern Photography* and *Popular Photography*—and read them cover-to-cover. For the first month or two their contents made about as much sense to me as *Finnegan's Wake* in Sanskrit. Gradually, as I got a handle on photographic nomenclature, both of these publications started to make sense—lots of sense.

At the same time I was acquainting myself with the photographic media, I was buttonholing every photographer and writer I knew who had sold photos to magazines. I needed to know what equipment would be best suited to my purposes.

I received much disparate advice about camera types, brands, models and lenses. As varied as the information was, most of it pointed in a single direction—toward a 35mm SLR with a fairly fast lens.

SLR stands for single-lens reflex, which means that the photographer, by putting his eye to the viewfinder, can see directly through the lens. This has the obvious advantage of allowing the picturetaker to see almost exactly what he is going to shoot.

The 35mm SLR offers a long list of other bonuses for the writer/photographer. First and foremost, it is light, easily transportable, and can be readied for use in a matter of seconds. For all-around versatility, it simply can't be beat. Virtually all SLRs on the market have interchangeable lenses whose capabilities range from ultra-wide ones that give panoramic fisheye effects, to hyperpowerful telescopic jobs that will bring a far-away object to within kissing distance. Similarly, 35mm SLRs offer their owners a wide choice of film, including those for color prints and slides, all manner of b&w, and even esoteric infrared. Better yet, the film is available at reasonable prices in stores from Topeka to Timbuktu.

Last, but surely not least, the innards of most SLRs contain many sophisticated space-age technological advances such as microminiaturized circuitry and sensitive light-metering cells. These components make it almost impossible for even unmechanical dolts like myself to snap a truly bad picture.

With the type of camera I needed established, the next problem was to pick one. This wasn't an easy chore in view of the fact that there are 100-plus brands and models available, a good 90% of which originate in the Land of the Rising Sun.

Price, obviously, was of paramount importance to me, and the pricing of photographic equipment, I quickly discovered, would confuse a full firm of Philadelphia lawyers. After considerable study I concluded there were five different pricing structures—manufacturers' list price, small town price, city price, discount price, and discount-discount price. In order to uncomplicate a complicated situation, let's take these one at a time.

Manufacturers' list price is just that—the price computed by the manufacturer. To my knowledge no retailer has ever had the unmitigated gall to charge these outrageous prices. Some latter-day Jesse Jameses, however, come mighty close. In small towns where there is only one camera store, some proprietors will shave a few—usually very few—percentage points from the list price and inform their customers they are getting a bargain. Strangely, many believe this. P.T. Barnum had a word for such people. It still applies!

In cities where there are several camera shops, competition exists, but in no way does it prevail. Here you can expect mark-downs ranging from 15 to 20%. In the same communities, you're likely to find so-called discount houses that number camera departments among their many appendages. You'll likely get discounts of 25% to 30% in these establishments and, unless you're exceedingly cautious, you may get something you weren't shopping for—the shaft! In recent years, many of these bargain bazaars have become the dumping grounds for discontinued lines and junk that no self-respecting camera store would handle. Moreover, most sales personnel that inhabit these dens of cupidity have roughly the same knowledge about things photographic as a bishop does about running a brothel.

Finally, we come to the discount-discounters. These exist only in our largest cities, but this is no problem because they do a huge mail-order business. No matter where you live you can avail yourself of the 40 to 50% discounts you'll get when you buy from these outfits. Each and every month their advertisements appear in the mail order sections of *Modern Photography, Popular Photography* and other photography magazines. Their offerings include practically every photographic item known to mortal man. Ordering from them is easy; most have toll-free telephone numbers. Thus, if you have a telephone and a credit card, your order can be on its way to you in a matter of hours.

Will you get what you order? You can bet on it! The bulk of the discount-discounters' business comes from their mail order operations, and, naturally, they want to keep you happy because they want you as a steady customer. Additionally, magazines in which these businesses advertise have mail order advertising codes nearly as strict as a Papal edict.

A few words of caution: When you buy from these organizations be sure you know what you really want. Some operate on a no-return, no-refund basis, unless, of course, the merchandise arrives at your door in damaged condition. The reasoning behind this policy is sound. In years gone by some less-than-honest photographer would order a pile of equipment, take it on assignment and then return it when the assignment was finished. This doesn't happen any more.

Breaking in Your Camera

OK. I knew the type of camera I needed and I knew where I could get the biggest bang for my hard-earned bucks, so what did I end up with?

The camera I ordered was made by a well-known Japanese manufacturer and it was at the low-end of their rather expensive line. While it wasn't the hottest camera that I could have gotten for the money, it came with a solid warranty and the distributor maintained several repair facilities around the country. Along with the camera, which came with a 50mm f2 lens, I ordered a 135mm f3.5 telephoto lens, a 2X teleconverter, a tripod, and a carrying case.

The cost was a shade under $275. Because of the current cut-throat competition among Japanese camera manufacturers, a comparable outfit would cost less today!

If a couple hundred bucks is still a bit out of your range, you can always try to find a good deal on a used camera. But beware—you can get burned if you don't know what you're doing. Before buying a used camera, be sure to shoot a few rolls of film through it to see how the prints turn out.

When my new equipment arrived I didn't rip into the package like a kid opening a Christmas present. Rather, I extracted the accompanying instruction booklets and read them carefully—not once but three times. Even though they were easily understandable, one or two points bothered me, so that evening I hastened over to the house of a friend who is something of a photography freak and had her give me a detailed explanation.

Within a day or two I was taking passably fair pictures and in less than a month, I'd sold my first two stories-cum-photos to a couple front-rank magazines I'd never been able to crack before.

If I've made photography sound easy, let me assure you it isn't quite that simple. It took me a good two years to obtain anywhere near the full potential from the relatively unsophisticated equipment I owned in those days.

If I were just getting into photography today, I'd do things somewhat differently. I'd take a correspondence course, for instance. Don't laugh! There are three or four truly excellent ones. I've seen their materials and instruction, and, believe me, by becoming a student with any of them, I could have learned more in six months than I did in two years using my "snap and be sorry" method. Another practical, inexpensive way to learn photography is to take an adult education course in the subject if your local school system is offering one.

The Payoff

Let's take a fast look at how that original $275 investment in photographic equipment has paid off over the years.

The first thing it did was open hundreds—yes, hundreds—of markets that had previously been off-limits to me. It also changed my entire approach to writing. Rather than getting an idea for a story and then trying to match it to a publication before writing it, my new *modus operandi* is a complete reversal.

I now take the photos, write the story, and then rummage through Writer's Market to pick out likely markets. Instead of coming up with one or two markets, I frequently compile a list of five to 15 magazines that are potential purchasers. (After all, I can now try those photos with manuscripts.)

This multiple choice of markets has had a salutary effect on my income. If a piece is rejected by one publication, I send it to another. Because of this, the number of manuscripts that I've finally had to relegate to my "file and forget" drawer has almost, but not quite, reached zero. Last year it was one and I blame my timing for its demise.

The quality of my writing also seems improved. The reason, I suspect, is the new freedom I find in not having to adhere to a single magazine's style and editorial taboos.

Since equipping myself with a camera, the number and frequency of my assignments has grown tremendously. I'd love to tell you that this profitable state-of-affairs has resulted from my sheer genius as a nonfiction writer. Alas, I'd be lying through my not-so-pearly teeth if I did.

What occasions this marked increase in my workload is pure economics. Because of skyrocketing postage and production costs, virtually every magazine editor in the country is working on a constricted editorial budget. Thus, it can save considerable money if an editor sends one person out on an assignment to do *both* the writing and photography.

Two other publishing trends have also contributed mightily to my financial well-being. I'm referring to the current insatiable demand on the part of many editors for "how-to" and "profile" pieces. To sell either type article without photos is sometimes tough, although there are magazines like *People* where the Powers That Be feel a good writer cannot be a good photographer—so you either have to be one or the other. On the other hand, good photos accompanying even a marginal article in either genre will invariably tilt the scales in favor of a check.

A camera, I've found, will frequently trigger a salable story idea. While taking a photo, for instance, I look at the subject much more closely than I normally would and start asking myself: "What?" "How?" "Why?" Checking through my files, I find my camera has acted as the *deus ex machina* for more than 40 sales in less than four years. Overall, I think that by learning to use a camera, I've *doubled* my story sales and *tripled* my income!

It's up to you to decide whether to take up photography. If you've set your sights on becoming a successful freelancer though, I don't see how you can afford not to.

Appendix A

Magazines: From the Beginning

The progenitor of magazines was an English gentleman, Edward Cave. In 1731, Cave got the idea that the world was ready for a publication that, in addition to news items and reviews, would include essays, fiction, poetry, and even some humor. The new periodical, which was printed in the newspaper format of that day, was called *Gentlemen's Magazine.*

Magazine meant *store house* and Cave had applied the term figuratively to his new publication. The name stuck even though some scholars and publishers still argue whether this now generic term is an apt one.

Readers didn't exactly kick the doors of Cave's print shop down in order to subscribe to his new magazine. In fact, the excitement magazines generated in literary circles was even less. Alexander Pope defined early magazines as "upstart collections of dullness, folly and so on."

It took ten years for Cave's new publishing idea to journey across the Atlantic to the colonies. Strangely, when the idea finally arrived on these shores, the first two American magazines were issued within three days of one another.

According to historians, Benjamin Franklin planned the first one. But, then as now, there was competition. A rival Philadelphia publisher, Andrew Bradford, anticipated Franklin's publication and got *American Magazine or a Monthly View of the Political State of the British Colonies* into the bookstalls on February 13, 1741. Franklin followed with his *General Magazine and Historical Chronicle for all British Publications in America* three days later. Both magazines were dated January 1741. Even in this early era publishers were tinkering with publication dates!

Neither of these magazines enjoyed any singular success. Bradford's magazine expired after three months and Franklin's bit the dust in six. The reason—or at least the basic reason—for the demise of both was their high price. The price of each was a sterling shilling, while the going daily wages of a skilled artisan was two shillings. Few Americans were willing to lay down half a day's pay for a magazine even though it contained a story on the Second Coming—which, incidentally, was a popular topic in early magazines.

Flat on Their Faces

The early history of magazines in this country is a dismal one. From 1741 to 1794, a grand total of 45 magazines were started. Unfortunately, a startling 60 percent of them did not last out their first year. Only four reached the ripe old age of three-and-a-half-years, while four of the periodicals died aborning during their first month of publication. Noah Webster, who was a great lexicographer, but not-so-great magazine publisher, summed up the situation when he said, "The expectation of failure is connected to the very name of a *magazine.*"

In addition to high production costs that necessitated high subscription rates, early magazine publishers faced myriad other problems. The low literacy rate in the colonies severely limited the number of readers, while transportation and the postal services were so poor that distribution was confined to small geographic areas. Because of this, circulation of any magazine was always low and, in many cases, miniscule. The largest circulation achieved by an American magazine during the 1700s was 1,500. This "mass circulation" was gained by Thomas Paine's *Pennsylvania Magazine* in 1776. The fact that there were a few momentous events that year no doubt hyped "Citizen Tom's" circulation.

Advertisers weren't of any measurable help to early magazine publishers. To begin with, there weren't many of them and the few that existed preferred to do their huckstering in the local newspapers. Finally, magazine publishers had a devil of a time filling their pages. The problem here was a shortage of writers—imagine that.

Somehow, magazines survived and took on an added dimension when a few perceptive publishers started periodicals directed toward special interest groups rather than the general public. The first magazine to pay special attention to women was published in Boston in 1784. A theatrical review appeared in 1798 and in 1802 the first humor magazine became available. Professional journals made their debut in 1808 with the appearance of the *American Law Journal.* By 1810 the first agricultural magazines were on the presses.

Up to this point, publishers had printed what they pleased. The consequences, if there were any, for printing a story that ruffled an individual's sensibilities was a duel or a tar and feathering. In 1811, however, this state of affairs came to an abrupt halt. That year, Dr. Benjamin Rush, famed Philadelphia surgeon, sued a magazine for libel and was awarded the then astronomical amount of $5,000. Publishers quickly became much more circumspect about what they printed.

Civil War Sparks Habit

For the first half of the 19th Century, magazines tottered along in a fitful fashion. Then came the American Civil War, an event that gave magazines a giant push forward.

Virtually every family in the divided republic had a son or sons fighting in the conflict, so there was an insatiable desire to know what was going on. Because of limited financial resources, coverage of the war by small local newspapers was scrimpy at best, and news of an important battle frequently appeared in print long weeks after it had been fought.

One magazine, *Harper's Weekly,* moved quickly to fill this informational void. It dispatched the best writers it could hire to cover the war and personalities fighting it. Whenever possible, dispatches were filed via telegraph to the magazine's headquarters within hours after the event. The stories were quickly edited, set in type, and frequently illustrated by teams of skilled wood engravers. Because of the magazine's weekly publishing frequency, the account, together with illustrations of recent events, could be in the reader's hands within a reasonable period of time. The editorial format developed by *Harper's Weekly* is still used by many successful publishers. But, more important than its trend-setting format, this magazine imbued large numbers of Americans with the *habit* of buying and reading magazines.

Magazine publishing came of age after the Civil War, due to many unrelated factors. First and foremost was a surge of technological advances in the graphic arts field. High speed presses were developed, Mergenthaler invented the Linotype and papermakers discovered countless ways to make their products cheaper. This meant that magazine publishers could sell their products for less and, thus, increase their circulation.

While this was happening, the railroad builders were pushing their rails into virtually every nook and cranny in the country. At the same time the efficiency of the Postal Service was climbing markedly. For publishers, this was a godsend. Now they could distribute copies of their magazines over vast geographical areas to thousands of subscribers at relatively low cost.

Finally, large numbers of advertisers discovered that magazines were an unusually effective and economical medium for promoting their products. With these additional revenues, the nation's magazine publishers were off and running!

Appendix B

Proofreading Symbols

Proofreading isn't a task that most writers get enthralled about, but it's a job that has to be done. Before you send out your manuscripts, read them at least twice and pencil in corrections *neatly*. The other occasion when you will be called upon to do proofreading is when editors send you galley proofs for your corrections. Read these carefully—it'll be the last time you'll have a chance to make any changes in your story before publication—and return them to the editor as quickly as possible. (Not all editors will send the author galley proofs, however, so you may or may not see your work before it appears in print.)

You'll look more professional and it will be a big help to both the editor and printers if you use these standardized proofreader's marks:

Symbol	Meaning		Symbol	Meaning
ℓ	Take out		?/	Insert question mark
stet	Let it stand		!/	Insert exclamation
#	Insert space		(/)	Insert parenthesis
⌒	Close up entirely		[/]	Insert brackets
tr	Transpose		*lc*	Lower case
sc or ⎓	Small capitals		¶	Paragraph
c+sc or ⎓	Caps and small caps		[	Move left
caps or ⎓	Capitals		]	Move right
V	Insert apostrophe		*Ital.*	Italic
⊙	Period		*or* —	
,/	Comma		*bf*	Bold face
:/	Colon		⊓	Move up
;/	Semicolon		⊔	Move down
❝ ❞	Quotation marks		*no* ¶	No paragraph
=/	Insert hyphen		*ℓ#*	Take out space

Example

¶ Posters, billbaords, highway signs, newspaper and magazine
headlines and advertising and the optometrist's eye examination
charts are usully done in sans serif or square serif letters.
    Sans serif includes two widely different types of letters. Gothic, as
most commonly seen in newspaper headlines, is the older variety of
sans serif. In the past twenty years or so many "new" sans serif faces
have come into wide usage.

Appendix C

Writer's "Rights"

When you sell an article to a publication, you should know exactly what rights you are selling. If the publisher doesn't tell you, find out before you cash the manuscript check—or preferably, before you send your manuscript to the publisher. Read the magazine's listing in *Writer's Market* or ask the editor to find out this information.

Some manuscript checks carry a printed release on the back that says, "all rights." Magazines that do buy all rights become the sole owner of your work, and can thus sell your story to anyone they please—such as movie and TV producers or other magazines. The writer has forfeited the right to use the story, in its present form, elsewhere. And remember—under the law, the publisher is not obligated to pay the original author any portion of the fee from these additional sales.

Most publishers buy "first serial rights" or "first North American serial rights," which gives them the right to print the story once. When a publication buys first North American serial rights, they are buying the right to publish first in both the U.S. and Canada. (This is sometimes important to a publisher whose magazine is distributed in Canada as well as the U.S.)

If a publisher buys first serial rights on one of your stories, and you subsequently find another buyer, you will need to write the original purchaser to ask for return of all other rights to your story. (He has been holding these rights in trust for you.) His letter officially transfers these rights back to you.

Second serial or "reprint" rights are what the editor who is publishing your story for the second time buys. The term "simultaneous rights" refers to a story being sold simultaneously to two or more magazines. About the only type of magazines that buy and publish on a simultaneous basis are religious publications—since their audiences usually don't overlap. In this case, the publisher would be printing a story that might also be scheduled to appear in another magazine at about the same time. (He would, of course, be aware of the simultaneous sale and approve of it.) For example, the editor of a Catholic magazine might not mind if a certain Christmas story was also going to appear in a Baptist publication—since his readers most likely would not even see the other publication. You will be selling "foreign serial rights" if you sell a story originally published in the U.S. to a publication in another country.

Copyright

Let's assume a story of yours is going to appear in a publication that isn't copyrighted. (To find out whether a magazine is copyrighted, you can either check *Writer's Market* or look for the copyright notice in the actual publication. The notice is usually near the bottom of the contents page.)

If your work is published in an uncopyrighted publication, it will fall into the public domain and will then be free for anyone to use. At that point, you would not be able to obtain a copyright on the work and it would have to be substantially revised for you to be able to get a copyright.

This doesn't mean you have to avoid uncopyrighted magazines, though, because you can copyright your work yourself. Simply ask the editor to publish the copyright symbol or the words *copyrighted by,* your name, and the date near your story. Fill out the "Contribution to a Periodical" form (available from the Copyright Office) and return it, with two copies of the published article and a check for the registration fee of $10.

For additional information, write the Copyright Office, Library of Congress, Washington DC 20559.

Index

Books of Interest From Writer's Digest

Art & Crafts Market, edited by Lynne Lapin and Betsy Wones. Lists 4,498 places where you can show and sell your crafts and artwork. Galleries, competitions and exhibitions, craft dealers, record companies, fashion-related firms, magazines that buy illustrations and cartoons, book publishers and advertising agencies — they're all there, complete with names, addresses, submission requirements, phone numbers and payment rates. 672 pp. $10.95.

The Beginning Writer's Answer Book, edited by Kirk Polking, Jean Chimsky, and Rose Adkins. "What is a query letter?" "If I use a pen name, how can I cash the check?" These are among 567 questions most frequently asked by beginning writers — and expertly answered in this down-to-earth handbook. Cross-indexed. 270 pp. $7.95.

The Cartoonist's and Gag Writer's Handbook, by Jack Markow. Longtime cartoonist with thousands of sales reveals the secrets of successful cartooning — step by step. Richly illustrated. 157 pp. $7.95.

A Complete Guide to Marketing Magazine Articles, by Duane Newcomb. "Anyone who can write a clear sentence can learn to write and sell articles on a consistent basis," says Newcomb (who has published well over 3,000 articles). Here's how. 248 pp. $6.95.

The Confession Writer's Handbook, by Florence K. Palmer. A stylish and informative guide to getting started and getting ahead in the confessions. How to start a confession and carry it through. How to take an insignificant event and make it significant. 171 pp. $6.95.

The Craft of Interviewing, by John Brady. Everything you always wanted to know about asking questions, but were afraid to ask — from an experienced interviewer and editor of *Writer's Digest.* The most comprehensive guide to interviewing on the market. 256 pp. $9.95.

The Creative Writer, edited by Aron Mathieu. This book opens the door to the real world of publishing. Inspiration, techniques, and ideas, plus inside tips from Maugham, Caldwell, Purdy, others. 416 pp. $6.95.

The Greeting Card Writer's Handbook, by H. Joseph Chadwick. A former greeting card editor tells you what editors look for in inspirational verse . . . how to write humor . . . what to write about for conventional, studio and juvenile cards. Extra: a renewable list of greeting card markets. Will be greeted by any freelancer. 268 pp. $6.95.

A Guide to Writing History, by Doris Ricker Marston. How to track down Big Foot — or your family Civil War letters, or your hometown's last century — for publication and profit. A timely handbook for history buffs and writers. 258 pp. $8.50.

Handbook of Short Story Writing, edited by Frank A. Dickson and Sandra Smythe. You provide the pencil, paper, and sweat — and this book will provide the expert guidance. Features include James Hilton on creating a lovable character; R.V. Cassill on plotting a short story. 238 pp. $6.95.

Law and The Writer, edited by Kirk Polking and Attorney Leonard S. Meranus. Don't let legal hassles slow down your progress as a writer. Now you can find good counsel on libel, invasion of privacy, fair use, plagiarism, taxes, contracts, social security, and more — all in one volume. 265 pp. $9.95.

Magazine Writing Today, by Jerome E. Kelley. If you sometimes feel like a mouse in a maze of magazines, with a fat manuscript check at the end of the line, don't fret. Kelley tells you how to get a piece of the action. Covers ideas, research, interviewing, organization, the writing process, and ways to get photos. Plus advice on getting started. 300 pp. $9.95.

The Mystery Writer's Handbook, by the Mystery Writers of America. A howtheydunit to the whodunit, newly written and revised by members of the Mystery Writers of America. Includes the four elements essential to the classic mystery. A clear and comprehensive handbook that takes the mystery out of mystery writing. 275 pp. $8.95.

One Way to Write Your Novel, by Dick Perry. For Perry, a novel is 200 pages. Or, two pages a day for 100 days. You can start — and finish — *your* novel, with the help of this step-by-step guide taking you from the blank sheet to the polished page. 138 pp. $6.95.

Photographer's Market, edited by Melissa Milar and Bill Brohaugh. Contains what you need to know to be a successful freelance photographer. Names, addresses, photo requirements, and payment rates for 1,616 markets. Plus, information on preparing a portfolio, basic equipment needed, the business side of photography, and packaging and shipping your work. 408 pp. $9.95.

The Poet and the Poem, by Judson Jerome. A rare journey into the night of the poem — the mechanics, the mystery, the craft and sullen art. Written by the most widely read authority on poetry in America, and a major contemporary poet in his own right. 482 pp. $7.95 ($4.95 paperback).

Stalking the Feature Story, by William Ruehlmann. Besides a nose for news, the newspaper feature writer needs an ear for dialog and an eye for detail. He must also be adept at handling off-the-record remarks, organization, grammar, and the investigative story. Here's the "scoop" on newspaper feature writing. 314 pp. $9.95.

A Treasury of Tips for Writers, edited by Marvin Weisbord. Everything from Vance Packard's system of organizing notes to tips on how to get research done free, by 86 magazine writers. 174 pp. $5.95.

Writer's Digest. The world's leading magazine for writers. Monthly issues include timely articles, interviews, columns, tips to keep writers informed on where and how to sell their work. One year subscription, $12.

Writer's Market, edited by Jane Koester and Bruce Joel Hillman. The freelancer's Bible, containing 4,454 places to sell what you write. Includes the name, address and phone number of the buyer, a description of material wanted and how much the payment is. 912 pp. $13.95.

Writer's Yearbook, edited by John Brady. This large annual magazine contains how-to articles, interviews and special features, along with analysis of 500 major markets for writers. $2.75 (includes 80¢ for postage and handling).

Writing and Selling Non-Fiction, by Hayes B. Jacobs. Explores with style and know-how the book market, organization and research, finding new markets, interviewing, humor, agents, writer's fatigue and more. 317 pp. $7.95.

Writing and Selling Science Fiction, compiled by the Science Fiction Writers of America. A comprehensive handbook to an exciting but oft-misunderstood genre. Eleven articles by top-flight sf writers on markets, characters, dialog, "crazy" ideas, world-building, alien-building, money and more. 191 pp. $7.95.

Writing for Children and Teen-agers, by Lee Wyndham. Author of over 50 children's books shares her secrets for selling to this large, lucrative market. Features: the 12-point recipe for plotting, and the Ten Commandments for writers. 253 pp. $8.95.

Writing Popular Fiction, by Dean R. Koontz. How to write mysteries, suspense thrillers, science fiction, Gothic romances, adult fantasy, Westerns and erotica. Here's an inside guide to lively fiction, by a lively novelist. 232 pp. $7.95.

(Add 50¢ for postage and handling.
Prices subject to change without notice.)
Writer's Digest Books, Dept. B, 9933 Alliance Road, Cincinnati, Ohio 45242